ENGLAND'S SECULAR SCRIPTURE

New Directions in Religion and Literature

Series Editors: Mark Knight, Roehampton University and
Emma Mason, University of Warwick

This series aims to showcase new work at the forefront of religion
and literature through short studies written by leading and rising
scholars in the field. Books will pursue a variety of theoretical
approaches as they engage with writing from different religious and
literary traditions. Collectively, the series will offer a timely critical
intervention to the interdisciplinary crossover between religion and
literature, speaking to wider contemporary interests and mapping
out new directions for the field in the early twenty-first century.

ENGLAND'S SECULAR SCRIPTURE

ISLAMOPHOBIA AND THE PROTESTANT AESTHETIC

JO CARRUTHERS

NEW DIRECTIONS IN RELIGION AND LITERATURE

continuum

Continuum International Publishing Group
The Tower Building   80 Maiden Lane
11 York Road   Suite 704
London SE1 7NX   New York NY 10038

www.continuumbooks.com

British Library Cataloguing-in-Publication Data
A catalogue record for this book is available from the British Library.

ISBN: 978-08264-3913-0 (hardcover)
978-08264-3321-3 (paperback)

Library of Congress Cataloging-in-Publication Data
A catalog record for this book is available from the Library of Congress

Typeset by Newgen Imaging Systems Pvt Ltd, Chennai, India
Printed and bound in Great Britain

CONTENTS

ACKNOWLEDGEMENTS

Thanks must first go to the Series Editors Mark Knight and Emma Mason who first thought that a book on Englishness and Protestantism was a good idea, and without whom it may never have been written. Unremittingly supportive, they have undoubtedly enriched this book by commenting on its early drafts. I am indebted to the Research Councils UK, who funded my Research Fellowship. I am also grateful to David Avital and Colleen Coalter at Continuum for bringing it to publication.

This book has been brewing for a long time and there are many people to thank for contributing towards it and for helping me refine my ideas. It is in conversations with Naomi Baker, alongside whom I first taught early modern literature at Manchester University, that the kernel of this book first started to take shape. I owe to her and my fellow postgraduates – especially Deirdre Boleyn, Rachael Gilmour and Zoë Kinsley – a debt of gratitude for support and friendship. My thoughts about Englishness were also helped along by the undergraduates at Lancaster University who took my course on 'England and Englishness'. They brought the many texts we studied to life and made me think more deeply about emotional attachment to nation. I have been extremely fortunate in my places of work and I thank my current colleagues at the University of Bristol in both the English and Theology departments, and those involved in the Place and Space theme, all of whom provide a collegial and stimulating research context.

My profound thanks go to all those who have generously commented on drafts: Naomi Baker, Sally Bushell, Ranji Devadason, Nasar Meer, Angela Piccini, Tom Sperlinger and Ika Willis. Many of my ideas have been formed over conversations with friends and colleagues, especially: Jeanette Brejning, Daniel Pablo Garay, Vivienne Jackson, Jon Roberts, Helen Smith, Catherine Spooner, Andrew Tate. I owe an especial debt of gratitude to those colleagues who have been unremittingly encouraging and wise: to Gavin D'Costa and Carolyn Muessig for being amazing, and to Angela, Ika, Ranji and Tom for friendship and collaborations.

My profound gratitude goes to my family. To my mum and John, thank you for moving to Skye and providing me with such a congenial working place! To Sue and Jeff for all your encouragement. To Richard, who has patiently supported the long hours that have gone into this book, thank you for your love, belief and practical support. And to Molly, whose support has been markedly less practical but who made my breaks more frequent and more fun.

SERIES EDITORS' PREFACE

This series of short monographs seeks to develop the long-established relationship between the disciplines of religion and literature. We posit that the two fields have always been intimately related, aesthetically, formally and theoretically, creating a reciprocal critical awareness framed by the relatively recent theo-literary thinking of figures such as Walter Benjamin, Martin Buber, Hans-Georg Gadamer and Geoffrey Hartman. Committed to reflecting on the question of how these two disciplines continue to interact, we are particularly concerned to redress the marked evasion of this relationship within existing scholarship. As Stanley Fish recently declared, religion has the capacity to 'succeed high theory and race, gender and class as the centre of intellectual energy in academe'. The books in this series are written by a group of critics eager to contribute to and read work intimate with both evolving and new religious and literary debates. Pursuing a variety of theoretical approaches to an array of literary and cultural texts, each study showcases new work on religion and literature while also speaking to wider contemporary concerns with politics, art and philosophy. In doing so, the books collectively map out new directions for the field in the early twenty-first century.

Mark Knight
Emma Mason

INTRODUCTION

In Frances Hodgon Burnett's *The Secret Garden* (1911)[1], the children sit in their newly restored garden, bursting to express their sense of celebration. Ben the gardener suggests they sing the Doxology hymn, even though 'He had no opinion of the Doxology and he did not make the suggestion with any particular reverence' (p. 233). Himself reluctant or ignorant, Ben proposes Dickon as singer, who explains 'They sing it i' church'. Colin, the group's leader, accepts the hymn as an expression of an unspecific sublimity: 'Perhaps it means just what I mean when I want to shout out that I am thankful to the Magic'. Dickon naturalizes it with his story that his mother 'believes th' skylarks sings it when they gets up i' th' mornin' (p. 234). The children imitate a church ritual as Dickon insists they take off their caps with Ben 'half-resentful', 'as if he didn't know exactly why he was doing this remarkable thing' (p. 234). The company sings the verse repeatedly, and Ben finally joins in, 'staring and winking and his leathery old cheeks were wet' (p. 235). Because it is written in full in the novel, the reader is also impelled to perform the Doxology internally:

> *Praise God from whom all blessings flow,*
> *Praise Him all creatures here below,*
> *Praise Him above ye Heavenly Host,*
> *Praise Father, Son, and Holy Ghost.*
> > *Amen.* (p. 234)

Written in the 1670s by Church of England Priest, Thomas Ken, the explicitly Trinitarian hymn is nonetheless vague enough to fulfil the childrens' less specific sentiments. At the heart of this quintessentially English story of simple joy in nature, then, is a dormant Protestantism that is awakened through its ritual enacting.

The garden trope itself is both English and Protestant, a reworking of a recourse to Eden and the desire to return to prelapsarian innocence and authenticity. In his *Identity of England*, in a chapter on Englishness and the country garden, Robert Colls notes that the garden in this story is 'recuperative of the spirit', a vitality that for David Gervais is tellingly English and identified in the Wordsworthian 'healing power' of nature.[2] A Protestantism that 'makes sense' and yet impels 'no particular reverence' lies at the heart of the recuperative English landscape in *The Secret Garden* and secular myths of Englishness alike. In the garden scene Protestantism is occult: magical, vague and beyond apprehension. It is occult in Englishness too. It acts magically, its workings unseen, inexplicable and mysterious to the English themselves.

As this book aims to show, the English simple life communicates a specifically Protestant impulse of simplicity that has a dual force. Innocent, straightforward and reviving, the garden heals the children emotionally, spiritually and physically, turning them into active and vibrant English children. The garden trope promotes an appealing simple life of spiritual sustenance, then, but it also presents an island state that's safe and secure, manicured and controlled. The garden's boundaries enclose and protect those inside, strengthening the group's identity. While the garden works to attenuate identity, it also creates a boundary against the undesirable. Zygmunt Bauman cites the trope of gardening (alongside architecture and medicine) as a practice '*in the service of the construction of an artificial social order, through cutting out the elements of the present reality that neither fit the visualized perfect reality, nor can be changed so that they do*'.[3] The alien threatens, he claims, 'by blurring the boundary of the territory itself and effacing the difference between the familiar (right) and the alien (wrong) way of life'. The garden is, then, a space that specifically keeps out those identities that threaten those inside.

In this book I trace mythologies of English simplicity to their emergence in the literature of Reformation England and identify the continuation of the oppositional force of early Protestantism in secular myths. The English are simple, straightforward, basically honest, self-possessed, phlegmatic, self-controlled and rational, governed by law and constituted by rights dating back to Magna Carta, they are fundamentally free. This book makes central that first term, *simple*, and argues that, as a principle and an aesthetic (for the two are inseparable), simplicity – located in the English landscape – enables and sustains wider English characteristics. And it is simplicity, I argue, that is a peculiarly Protestant aesthetic and concept. As this intro-duction will go on to outline, simplicity while seemingly innocent and benign is an aesthetic and concept that perpetuates a Reformed antagonism and that informs an equally oppositional sense of Eng-lish identity.

The rest of this introduction introduces the book's intellectual context. I begin with a brief discussion of debates over Englishness and outline the centrality of aesthetics to my approach to English identity before giving a brief history of the significance of simplicity before and within the English Reformation that provides a context for the more detailed literary analysis of Chapter One. I then go on to define what I mean by 'Secular Scripture', a term that gestures towards the relationship between secularism, religion and rational-ism, and the centrality of English literature to enduring versions of English identity. The Introduction closes with an outline of the key methodological concepts: the relevance of the concept of mytholo-gies and how it explains the persistence of a Protestant force within a secular aesthetic of simplicity; and the interrelation between aesthet-ics and viscerality and their implications for the continuity of English identity.

ENGLISHNESS

The surge in studies and expressions of English identity over the past couple of decades has had various explanations: postcolonial self-questioning, the strengthening of internal UK borders because of devolution and the revival of the St. George flag in national cele-brations (or not) over football.[4] Debates over the definition of Eng-lishness are too varied to recount here. As a term that came into use only in 1805, its very terminology, and any historical trajectory, is certainly contested.[5] The 'modernist' position posits national iden-tity as emerging within the eighteenth-century Enlightenment, and as such it is asserted as a thoroughly secular entity and of recent formation.[6] In this book I follow theorists such as Adrian Hastings, Liah Greenfeld and Anthony Smith who look back to the early mod-ern era (and even earlier) for the emergence of national identity.[7] In recent use Englishness refers to the character of the people inhabit-ing the geographical space of England, but is nonetheless often con-flated with its larger political body, the United Kingdom, making it a highly contested term. Englishness is seen as both pre-existing Brit-ishness (for example in John Fowles) and as emerging only at the point of imperial disintegration (for example in Krishnan Kumar).[8] What is overwhelming in the popular nostalgic celebrations of Eng-lishness (that this book will largely be concentrating on) is precisely the problematic state of English identity. Once divine, a notion that led an Empire, the Englishness that many seek to acclaim has been defrocked, ripped apart by iconoclasts and bears the weight of an imperial and colonial litany of abuses. Jeremy Paxman cites the need to reclaim a lost confidence as his motivation for compiling his best-selling book on the English: 'Those countries who do best in the world – the ones that are safe and prosperous – have a coherent sense of their own culture'.[9] Cole Moreton's response is similarly nostalgic and anxious: 'We still look for a sense of community. We still love to be eccentric, from Morris dancers to Whovians (Doctors Who fans). We still believe in fair play. If we can find new ways to express these things we will keep the extremists at bay.'[10]

Distress calls over the loss of English identity are common in popular forums. John Sentamu, Archbishop of York, is representa-tive in his call for a return to traditional values in his speech on 'Eng-lishness', delivered at the *Sunday Times Literary Festival* in Oxford, 4 April 2009, reprinted a few days later in *The Sun*.[11] There he claimed that the English 'having shed an Empire, have also lost a noble vision for the future'. 'What do we really want for our beloved land?' he asks. Sentamu sees loss of Empire as creating a dangerous schism with England's past: 'Dissatisfaction with one's heritage creates an opening for extremist ideologies', he concludes. It is not merely dis-satisfaction but ignorance that needs addressing: 'We need to become better acquainted with this legacy, be grateful for it, rediscover its dynamic and build upon it.' Anxiety over the demise of an authentic English character has perhaps been fuelled by the denunciation of national identity as mythological in the academy that has exposed its shaky foundations. National identity has not escaped postmodern theory's exposure of the contingency and partiality of all attempts at self-identity. In his elegy for England, Roger Scruton considers Tom Nairn's and Perry Anderson's famous interrogation of national identity and its cultural traditions as disloyal, labelling it 'sneering and bitter'.[12] As the warnings against extremism indicate, intrinsic to laments over the demise of Englishness is a strong sense of national protectionism and fervour. They are evident especially in

expressions of xenophobic and most recently in anti-Islamic sentiment which seem to have at their disposal a firm sense, at least, of
what the English are not. This study does not seek to demystify Englishness in tracing its contingencies and constructions; instead an
acknowledgement of the force of (a nonetheless constructed) Englishness as a powerful influencer of attitude and action is central.
Even if myths of Englishness are not easily articulated and do not
map onto the everyday lives of English people, they are nonetheless
put to work in the alienation of certain individuals or groups.

THE PROTESTANT AESTHETIC

The most common way of conceptualizing Protestantism's heritage is
that the theological became secularized into a moral imperative, as
outlined in Max Weber's renowned theory of Puritan duty in *The Protestant Ethic*.[13] As George Orwell comments in his *The English People*
of 1947, most of the English would consider religion in moral terms:

> A vague theism and intermittent belief in life after death are prob-
> ably fairly widespread, but the main Christian doctrines have been
> largely forgotten. Asked what he meant by 'Christianity,' the aver-
> age man would define it wholly in ethical terms ('unselfishness,' or
> 'loving your neighbour,' [. . .]).[14]

The equation is convincing and no doubt true – in a modern age,
morality has thrown off what is considered to be the burden of its
theologically hewn attire. But this is only part of the story. This book
argues that theological doctrines were transposed not merely into a
moral register, but at a very early stage into an aesthetic register. And
it is in this aesthetic form that they have been able to remain dominant within articulations of Englishness from the early modern
period to today.

Unlike other theories of secularization that trace a 'history of ideas'
(such as those by Charles Schmitt and Charles Taylor), this book
looks instead to aesthetics as the site of Englishness's debt to Protestantism (although these aesthetics are often discursively articulated).[15]
Protestantism's influence is apparent, then, in the perpetuation of an
aesthetic that is no longer recognized as Protestant but that communicates the especially oppositional English-Protestant paradigm of
the post-Reformation period. This 'Protestant aesthetic' is subject,

just as discursive constructions of Englishness are, to the vicissitudes of time and cultural change. Yet precisely because the aesthetic perpetuates an unarticulated logic it is often not subject to rational opposition. Sinisterly, it continues in a non-rational realm (carrying with it a historically specific logic) and is therefore potentially more resilient than explicit rational articulation. It is the form of the aesthetic – and its complement of the discriminating reader – that acts as a proficient vehicle for the continuation of a religious logic to an apparently secular identity. It is in the particularly innocent form of simplicity that Protestant oppositional logic has continued into the present day to fuel antagonistic sentiment, as the following chapters seek to outline.

By transferring focus towards aesthetics this study hopes to counter the prevailing emphasis upon discourse and ideas in theories of national identity and to contribute to studies that emphasize the aesthetic, performative and visceral.[16] For theorists who look back to the early modern period, the debt is one of the emergence of a new idea or a discursive construction to which the group adheres: freedom for Linda Colley and Liah Greenfeld, a sense of mission for Anthony Smith and Hans Kohn.[17] The revolution and rejection of monarchal rule in the seventeenth century seems a fitting beginning of modern democracy, or as Colley puts it, a time when Englishmen, or rather English Protestants, 'still had access to the word of God in a way (they believed) that Roman Catholics did not, and for this reason, if for no other, Protestants, even the poorest of them, were free men' (*Britons,* p. 42). It has also become almost commonplace to locate modern notions of subjectivity and individualism in this period.[18] Many critics have been resistant to the concept of individuals as 'free and individual' emerging from 'religious thought', which they assert as oppressive and irrational. Greenfeld for one posits religion as separate from such notions: 'it was only natural that at the time of the centrality of religion in every sphere of social existence, nascent nationalism was clothed in religious idiom' (p. 63). In other words, new ideas of nationalism and proto-democracy are an essence onto which is draped an alien religious form. Such ideas may have emerged from a religious context, Greenfeld implies, but they are separate from it and easily shed all connection with it. As such the English have as their foundation 'no longer religion, but the national idea based on the liberty of the rational individual' (p. 73).[19]

Why has the Protestant impulse in contemporary Englishness been neglected? For many there can be little appeal in tracing oppositional articulations of Englishness back to its Reformed roots. On a theoretical level, it sounds hopelessly naïve to want to locate a present identity in an historical source, as though anything pure from the past has travelled into the present. However, the opposite position (although less obviously so) is equally naïve. The idea that present voices construct the past in their own image is both undeniable and impossible because it places a level of agency on the present individual that ignores dependence on past codes. It assumes an undue passivity for 'subaltern' voices (such a polarization of power is a common critique of Edward Said's theories of Orientalism).[20] There can be little appeal for either Protestant or Atheist to trace a religious influence: Protestantism's part to play in an antagonistic Englishness merely reveals historical flaws, while promoters of secularism are loathe to admit to their entanglements in religious logics and discourse.

This book posits, then, an aesthetic revolution in the sixteenth and seventeenth centuries in which simplicity took on the mantle of both Protestant theology and the new formation of Protestant English identity. Crispin Sartwell asserts the centrality of aesthetics in the period: 'the extent to which the Reformation and the Counter-Reformation, and for that matter Catholicism itself, are to be understood as essentially aesthetic movements is far underappreciated, even if accounts of these events almost always resort to works of art and acts of iconoclasm as emblems'.[21] His argument, like Christopher Hill's, is that art and events are not to be read merely in the light of each other but that 'the political, aesthetic, and religious expressions are not, in fact, distinguishable in any given embodiment' (p. 203).[22] The strong tie between theology, ideas and aesthetics in this period means that any specific aesthetic such as simplicity is imbued with theological significance. Yet the aesthetic bypasses linguistic rationality even though it still functions semiotically (pointing to a set of ideas or assumptions beyond itself). The aesthetic of simplicity is bound up specifically in Protestant hermeneutics of transparency. This relation may seem obvious because the link between simplicity and transparency is so intuitive to us now. But looking to formulations of simplicity before the Reformation, it becomes clear contemporary associations of simplicity are historically situated.

SIMPLICITY

Roger Scruton, writer of *England: An Elegy* (2000), rails against theorists who suggest national identity is a product of state and administrative convenience rather than an organic manifestation of group sentiment and affiliation. He turns for defence to simplicity. Such theories, he states, are 'seized upon with glee by those who find simple loyalties of simple people both dangerous and unattractive' (p. 4). The force of Scruton's meaning here depends on the assumption that the innocent, pleasing and benign qualities of simplicity are self-evident. How absurd, he implies, to find simplicity – simple loyalties and simple people – either dangerous or unattractive. Simplicity is a central tenet of Englishness for Scruton, although he rarely discusses it overtly and it is certainly not a term important enough for his index. He looks back to the Prayer Book as 'that extraordinary idiom' that 'enabled the English to express complex moral sentiments in direct and simple terms' (p. 99). Despite the horrors that the Baptist church presents with its 'terrible ordeal' of baptism, what manages to touch him is precisely the 'simple trust and piety' that he witnesses there (p. 89).

Scruton is representative in his simultaneous recourse to and explicit neglect of simplicity, which is perhaps the most prevalent and important characteristic in models of Englishness. The term 'simplicity' references the rhetorically straightforward and the aesthetically plain, both linked to moral purity; it also refers to the rustic, invoking a specifically rural sense of the simple life. Simplicity, then, carries a wealth of significance compared to its alternatives such as 'plain' and 'straightforward' (which are used as synonyms when relevant). While plain has an aesthetic emphasis, and straightforward a conceptual one, simplicity is a term that contains both emphases and even blurs them in its lack of specificity, implicating the visual within the conceptual and vice versa.

The meanings that we now attribute to the aesthetic and concept of simplicity are indebted to the transformation of the significance of simplicity in the early modern period. Simplicity became a signifier of English identity in a Reformation England in which simplicity took on a whole new set of associations.[23] Long before the sixteenth century, visual simplicity had been an important symbol within religious life in England. The plain habits of monks and nuns pointed to the wearer's aspiration, in life and attitude, to the ideal of Christ's humility. The plain and simple functioned within a complex nexus of religious signifiers: while monastic clothing spoke of humility, the ornate gold that was used in iconography, manuscripts and church vessels indicated Christ's divinity.[24] The Church Fathers venerated the simple style of the Scriptures, but in a way that was importantly distinct from the Reformers. For the Fathers, Scripture's simplicity was the chosen form of communication that spoke of God's efforts to speak to humankind on their own level. As Peter Auksi explains: 'Like the incarnation, the style of Scripture gives ordinary humanity some access to, or intelligible contact with, mysteries'.[25] The simplicity of form expressed, not belied, the complexity and distance of the divine to the human that the incarnation similarly demonstrated. As with monks' habits, simplicity for the Church Fathers signified merely one facet of a wider semiology: inextricably bound up with mystery, it expressed God's incarnational move towards humanity. Within theological discourse, as articulated most profoundly by Aquinas, simplicity meant primarily divine simplicity: the concept that God was unique and inimitable.[26] In theological terms, then, simplicity signified uniqueness and even the complexity and ineffableness of the divine.

At the Reformation – considered by its followers as a new age of purity and access to divine truth – simplicity came to signify most obviously the eschewing of Catholic ritual and ornamentation.[27] Although Protestantism was marked by intense aesthetic debates especially in its early manifestations and was by no means a homogenous religious movement, in its more durable articulations simplicity became a hallmark aesthetic of anti-Catholicism. As John King notes, 'Many Protestants interpreted the cleansing of the Temple [in which Christ removes traders] as a figure for the Reformation through the purgation of church ornamentation and external aids to devotion'.[28] Because the strongly visual and negative imperative of iconoclasm is pervasive in Reformed theologies, simplicity is often treated as a lack: as the paring down of Catholic elaborateness. It is thereby one expression of an anti-Catholic sentiment that was especially vehement in England. Pasi Ihaleinen's cross-national research has demonstrated that England, in contrast to its Protestant neighbours Sweden and the Netherlands, was especially anti-Catholic and oppositional in the sixteenth to eighteenth centuries.[29] This peculiar antagonism is apparent in Edmund Spenser's *The*

Faerie Queene, visualized in the duplicitous witch, Duessa. Her 'foule and hideous' (I.ii.41) body is enchanted so that she appears beautiful, but hers is the ostentatious beauty of the Whore of Babylon from Revelation 17, a figure whose regal appearance, in her 'gold and purple pall' (I.vii.16) is a sensuous spectacle symbolizing for Spenser's readers a corrupt and lascivious Catholic church.[30] As Naomi Baker succinctly explains: 'Denouncing what they perceived to be the worldly corruption of "papist" principles, Protestant reformers [. . .] rejected the deployment of visual stimuli in Christian worship, associating sensuous displays with corruption, pride and false religion.'[31] Iconoclasm enacted rejection of Rome and expressed a sense of English political freedom. Clement Fatoviç states that articulations of English liberty in political writings of the sixteenth to eighteenth centuries are overwhelmingly shaped by anti-Catholicism to the degree that 'Popery was paradigmatic of unfreedom itself' ('The Anti-Catholic Roots', p. 40).

Simplicity is commonly configured therefore through what it is not – in negative terms – a lack (of ostentation or ornament) rather than a positive definition. But simplicity also communicated a set of concrete theological assertions: belief in the transparency of Scripture, known widely as 'plain style', itself represented a theologically informed hermeneutical position towards Scripture, as well as the self and the world. The Bible was freed from what was perceived as medieval and Latinate obstruction, and the host – the body of Christ, once held aloft by the priest at some distance from the congregation – was now an accessible, touchable symbol of Christ's death. The mystery and magic that had surrounded Scripture and ritual had now become ordinary – the Bible was rendered in everyday language and the eucharist entered the personal realm of memorial. That the Bible and sacrament were straightforward and thereby accessible was central to the Reformers, who asserted the simplicity of the Scriptures that enabled the translation both of the divine to the human and of foreign languages into the vernacular. Luther, in his opening to his commentary on the Psalms, available in English translation in 1577, advocates the reading of the 'simple text' of Scripture, 'without further helpes' as it has 'matter enough to giue intelligence and instruction sufficient to the soule of man for saluation' (although he does praise God for 'commentaries & explications', which are nonetheless 'much requisite, & greatly needefull' to quench 'controuersies').[32] Calvin's writings, far more ubiquitous in England than Luther's,[33] locates singular interpretation within a simple Scripture: 'that there should bee one trew vnitie of fayth, so the simplicitie of the Gospell go before it and guyde it'.[34] The point for these Reformers was, as Thomas Luxon outlines, that 'all forms of misbelief and apostasy were understood as being produced by an inadequate understanding of the one true literal sense of God's revelation in Scripture'.[35] The obvious aesthetic counterpart to the opening up of Scripture was simplicity. While visual imagery was thought to mediate God's voice, the translucent Word rendered God present. The reforming impulse and simplicity seemingly went hand in hand.

The significance of simplicity changes at the Reformation because it takes on the paradigmatic force of transparency as a groundbreaking hermeneutic.[36] Although characterized by a move inward, to the individual and the conscience, Reformed Christianity is nonetheless outwardly fashioned according to aesthetic principles. Theologians such as William Dyrness have noted the inward turn of aesthetics at the Reformation. The 'image', newly defined in texts such as John Bale's influential commentary on Revelation *The Image of Both Churches*, became internalized.[37] The move inward heralded, Dyrness argues, 'a major shift in the use of the imagination' (p. 6). But Reformation theologies also had external expression. Spenser's *The Faerie Queene*, in fashioning the 'twelue priuate morall verutues', chooses to portray them in the 'image of a braue knight' that is here distinctly visual, the term brave indicating not merely courage but showiness or fine dress.[38] Spenser is drawing attention not merely to the internal characteristics of his knights (as one would expect), but to the visual significance of their outward apparel.[39] Spenser sets Redcrosse, his 'braue' knight of Book I, with the 'ornament' of a cross, utilizing language that may seem to signify Catholic ostentation but that becomes reconfigured to construct a specifically Protestant aesthetic that foregrounds simplicity. In her study of nationhood in Spenser, Shakespeare and Drayton, Claire McEachern argues that the key to understanding England's cohering nationhood is through the formal property of prosopopoeia – the rendering of the inanimate in anthropomorphic terms, so that, for example, 'Spenser portrays the church as an elusively chaste woman'. 'Embodied', she argues, 'the state becomes familiar [. . .] the prosopopoeitic gesture cultivates the intimate affect constitutive of corporate feeling'.[40] Prosopopoeia indeed renders the state familiar, but it also transforms

theological and political ideas (what the church should be, in specifically doctrinal terms) into an aesthetic (a clothed and outwardly
delineated figure). So, we find in Spenser and others the theological
rendered quite self-consciously in aesthetic terms. Spenser's Protestant apocalyptic world demonstrates to us just how aestheticized the
early modern religious world was, despite iconoclasm's seeming
opposition to the aesthetic (which labelled only certain materials as
icons or images).

The move from ornate Catholicism to the simplicity of Reformation aesthetics was not unproductive or uncreative. To conceive of
the process as the removal of the ornate outer garments of Catholicism to reveal a bare and unadorned, more truthful, core was, indeed,
how Protestants frequently articulated the move, but it is to under-
estimate the mythological character of Protestant simplicity. Instead
a set of Protestant aesthetics merely replaced another, Catholic, set
that was in many ways no less complex.[41] As King notes (elaborating
upon Stephen Greenblatt's description of the destruction of the
Bower of Bliss in *The Faerie Queene* book II as 'the principle of
regenerative violence', in which the 'act of tearing down is the act of
fashioning'), 'the internalization within *The Faerie Queene* of the
Reformation attack against idolatry is a force that is aesthetically
constructive as well as *destructive*' (*Spenser's Poetry*, p. 7). As Guyon's
violence regenerates, so the iconoclast principles and actions of the
Reformers constructed a whole new set of aesthetic associations.
Specific images were no longer the repository of divine communication and the ordinary material world became theophanic. As Dyrness
argues, 'Reformed Protestants, in ways analogous to other religious
traditions, developed an "imagination" that is a characteristic way of
laying hold of the world and of God that comes to expression in
their material (and especially their visual) culture'.[42] England's landscape, its manners, and its people – entwined with the aesthetic of
simplicity – all spoke of God's will and, most pertinently, Providence
for His chosen nation. And when the Protestant emphasis waned,
these elements of Englishness nonetheless persisted in the aesthetic
realm, as this book aims to demonstrate.

But simplicity as a signifier of only transparency does not
adequately explain its potency as a key signifier of Englishness. What
is important for the working of simplicity is its communication of
English superiority, a superiority tied to their identity as the Protestant elite. And it is this double force – Protestant and chosen – that

renders the Englishman's vision necessarily clear: only the English can truly discern. Simple aesthetics demand a reciprocal reader who recognizes simplicity's worth, a reader discerning enough not to be snared by the false beauties of ornament. A natural preference for the aesthetically simple is to suggest a preference for the morally simple, for truth and justice. As Chapter One outlines, the English's superior interpretive skills are related to the prioritization of rationality and the suppression of emotion considered necessary for discerning reading: the famous English reservation and self-possession. Simplicity, then, promoted a whole set of beliefs about English character. Simplicity, this book argues, *is* England's Protestant aesthetic in that it communicates, and carries forward in a neat package, Protestantism's new hermeneutical emphases.

SIMPLICITY: ENGLAND'S SECULAR SCRIPTURE

What the title of this book claims is that contemporary Englishness is still defined, in an oblique and distorted way admittedly, but defined nonetheless by the same Scriptural paradigm that defined it five hundred years ago. The title *England's Secular Scripture* attests to both the scripting of secular Englishness according to the Scriptural paradigms of Reformation theologies and the siting of Englishness in the literary canon (which I will discuss shortly). Northrop Frye in his *The Secular Scripture: A Study of the Structure of Romance* looks for a transferral of the cosmic claims of religion into the secular.[43] My title relates instead to the seeping of biblical and religious norms, myths and logics into secular narratives, and as such my project is to consider the slippage within secularity that reveals its imbrication with religious logic. This is not to say that the secular is somehow actually religious: secularism (L. *saecularis*, 'age' or 'generation') is defined by the deliberate expulsion of the spiritual and transcendent from the historical moment, from the material world. In *Paradise Lost* the Archangel Michael gives Adam a view of the future world: of the coming of Christ, salvation and the subsequent fall of the church into what Milton sees as 'truth/ With superstitions and traditions taint' (XII. 511–12) and speaks of such a church seeking 'Places and titles, and with these to join/ Secular power, though feigning still to act/ By spiritual' (XII. 516–7).[44] For Milton, secular and spiritual are polar opposites. Secularity is synonymous with 'carnal power', ambitious in material terms: it is the negative removal of a spiritual or righteous imperative that results in materialism, greed, selfishness. In contemporary usage, the secular is still that which is separated from or rejects religion, but in its most benign terms it suggests neutrality: a scientific, objective stance that is not swayed or influenced unduly by religious forces, but that liberally allows their existence on a personal level.[45] As T. N. Madan has outlined, secularism is associated with progress and since its inception as an idea it has 'retained a positive connotation'.[46] So, while for Milton it spelt disaster and moral deficiency, for many today it offers a welcome release from what is seen as an archaic and superstitious ideology and bias. Yet in neither definition is the religious a subcategory of the secular. Instead, they are more properly antithetical terms. Because the secular is at heart adverse to religion, it is the co-existence of the religious and the (anti-religious) secular that is provocative. What I mean by a secular Scripture, then, is the uneasy continuance of Scriptural tenets within the supposedly neutral but anti-religious secular realm.

What does this focus on the religious and secular mean for Englishness? To start with, it raises questions about the secularity of contemporary Englishness: how far can it be defined as a secular identity when parts of its logic are essentially non-secular, non-worldly, and are instead bound up with specifically religious formulations? Again, this is not to say that Englishness is better or more authentically conceived of as a religious identity. Instead, within the fabric of Englishness the threads of religious logic are those woven from a cloth of once-living faith. Supposedly 'secular' Englishness is a messy bricolage that includes the residual religious ideas, the corpses and ghosts of a past religious creed that are distant from living faith traditions. It is the corpse-like quality of these residual ideas that is problematic: they are carried forward, static and unchanging, bearing an influence that is unresponsive to dynamic life. Roland Barthes, poignantly, describes myth as 'speaking corpses'.[47] Such speaking corpses are dogmatic by nature. They are, ironically, secular in the literal sense of the term: of an age, of a generation, worldly. They are religious in the sense that they are reflective of a *system* that organizes expressions of belief and are, as such, static. But they are not spiritual and they are not relational, in the sense of a practice of the worship of a transcendent being or principle; they are not alive. Weber wrote in similar terms regarding the infamous Protestant work ethic: 'the idea of duty in one's calling prowls about in our lives like the ghost of dead religious beliefs' (*The Protestant Ethic*, p. 124). When it comes to English relations with religious identities other than Protestant, the activities of the corpse become pertinent. If secular Englishness is indebted to a specific form of religion, Reformed Protestantism, that was an essentially antagonistic self-identity, protesting, reforming and setting itself apart, then the danger is that secular Englishness is unwittingly partisan and antagonistic.

The problem of England's rooting in Protestant doctrines is not the continuation or transferral of beliefs into another order or paradigm, but the ghostly nature of such continuances. Not quite substantial, Protestant doctrines persist because they are unseen and unquestioned. Alongside the strength of attachment to Protestant values for English self-identification there is a concurrent lack of rational reflection on those attachments. This lack of acknowledgement is what enables the ghostly Protestant aesthetic and its mythologies to fuel antagonism.

Part of this book's interrogation of the religious/secular borderline is an interest in a wider critique that tests the limits of the claims of rationalism; a rationalism that is the logical bedfellow of secularism. Deconstructionist theorists have argued that rationalist and secular agendas have been impossible to implement because assumptions of transcendence are endemic in Western thinking.[48] The very impulse of secularization is premised on a belief in rationality to secure all areas of life, a belief that rational argument and thought can expunge the risky non-rational (that includes emotional, and religious impulses, thoughts and 'logics'). It is the belief in rationalism's ability to separate out, to attenuate, that is challenged in this book. In this way, rationalism's expulsion – or control over – the non-rational is analogous to the English celebration of self-possession: the ability of the Englishman to temper his passions, to be moderate and self-controlled; in short to be ruled by the intellect, not the body and its emotions. As seen in Bauman's interrogation of the garden trope, the simplicity and simple life signified in England-as-garden belies a rationalist agenda of pruning undesirable and aesthetically unfitting elements.

LITERATURE: ENGLAND'S SECULAR SCRIPTURE

This book's title also gestures towards the importance of the canon of English literature as a secular scripture which dates back at least to the canonization of Shakespeare and Milton at the beginning of the eighteenth century.[49] The continuance of simplicity and its carrying of a metaphysical-theological force (itself an outworking of the secularization of Reformed attitudes to the Scriptures), has been dependent upon the continuation of the literary canon as a secular Scripture. As a particular touchstone for Englishness, literature is the national medium. As Said contends, the liberal humanist culture of England (traced back for him to Matthew Arnold's analysis of culture, but potentially also to early modern writing) imposes an English, or imperial, cultural identity:

> You read Dante or Shakespeare in order to keep up with the best that was thought and known, and also to see yourself, your people, society, and tradition in their best lights. In time, culture comes to be associated, often aggressively, with the nation or the state; this differentiates 'us' from 'them', almost always with some degree of xenophobia. Culture in this sense is a source of identity, and a rather combative one at that.[50]

There is a repeatedly articulated sense that it is in literature that true English genius may be found. For J. B. Priestley, literature is central to a consideration of Englishness because it reveals the 'greatness' of the English that may be clouded in real life. 'Great' literature becomes both exemplary and representative: the English genius is thereby at once rare and ubiquitous. He situates the authentic representation of Englishness in literature:

> the English mind, where mirth and melancholy play like light and shadow, sunshine and mist; a mind that, once robbed of its bloom and golden haze, is utterly without charm, giving us the leaden-eyed Englishman of the satirists. Fortunately that bloom and that golden haze are there for ever in the long splendour of English literature.[51]

The writer is representative: 'they are Englishmen who have more vivacity of thought and greater powers of expression than their neighbours but whose minds work in the same way' (p. 10).

A symbol of national greatness, literature is also the site (alongside the liturgical,[52] domestic and everyday) in which the Protestant aesthetic took shape and coalesced into a national aesthetic. The rise of modern English literature occurred during Protestantism's ascendency, with some critics even reading authors such as Chaucer or Piers Plowman as 'proto-Protestant'.[53] Edmund Spenser's *The Faerie Queene* and John Milton's *Paradise Lost*, two of the most influential works from the sixteenth and seventeenth centuries, published nearly seventy years apart, render Protestant doctrine in self-consciously and carefully crafted aesthetic form. Simplicity in these works, explicitly doctrinal and Protestant, is nonetheless the first mode of secularization in the sense that it is rendered in a form separable from its religious foundation as it enters a 'worldly' form. As such, the literary tradition is central to the passing-on, and transposition of, Protestant theologies into the everyday of secular Englishness. And in the act of reading, literature's Protestant aesthetics are revived in contemporary secular concepts of England.

Literature also communicates the imaginary, an element recognized as vital to national identity since Benedict Anderson's *Imagined Communities* of 1983.[54] Literature reveals the imagined as central to the seemingly prosaic realities of life. As Gervais comments, 'Part of the novel's complexity is that it circumvents the facile juxtaposition of the real and the ideal, as if they belonged to different realms' (p. 5). In other words, literature (and the novel especially for Gervais), brings forward the imaginary and the material as intertwined entities. Literature communicates the 'imagined community', imagined and yet real, that vague and often non-explicit 'feeling' or 'sense' of identity, what Raymond Williams calls 'structures of feeling' which he describes as 'the actual living sense, the deep community that makes the communication possible'.[55] Literature is thereby a privileged site for identifying 'everyday Englishness' because of its depiction of the habitual details of everyday life. Never systematic, there are nonetheless discernible patterns of thought that can be articulated in a formal manner to resemble a 'structure'. Louis Althusser demonstrates the affective qualities of art:

> What art makes us *see*, and therefore gives to us in the form of '*seeing*', '*perceiving*', and '*feeling*' (which is not the form of *knowing*), is the *ideology* from which it is born, in which it bathes, from which it detaches itself as art, and to which it *alludes*.[56]

Althusser recognizes the inherently experiential nature of artistic works; works that inculcate knowledge which are themselves not 'the form of *knowing*'. In other words, artistic works communicate a knowledge that, although 'bathed' in an ideological context, make that context opaque, rendering it unseen. Alhusser's forms of seeing, perceiving and feeling are essentially visceral; they are allusional rather than consciously articulated. Because 'ideology slides into all human activity', he argues, 'it is identical with the "lived" experience of human existence itself: that is why the form in which we are "made to see" ideology in great novels has as its content the "lived" experience of individuals' (p. 152). The novel therefore presents the everyday, and because the everyday is the site of ideological work, the novel presents the 'feeling' of an ideology and gives us experience. But, as Althusser outlines, art does not present those ideologies for scrutiny. It instead deletes itself and renders itself unseen. He claims, quoting Spinoza, that 'art makes us "see" "conclusions without premisses [sic]"', whereas knowledge makes us penetrate into the mechanism which produces the '"conclusions" out of the "premisses" [sic]' (p. 153). 'Literature' (alongside 'the press, the radio and television') is numbered in his list of 'cultural ISAs', Ideological State Apparatuses, forms through which, in his schema, the state insidiously 'drums into' us (primarily through schooling) the ruling ideology, a way of bearing oneself, that perpetuates a way of believing and seeing the world. [57]

It is ubiquitous in celebrations of Englishness to quote John of Gaunt's 'sceptred Isle' speech from *King Richard II*. Invoking the triumphal poetry of the past bolsters a strong self-image and the glance backwards to the past, the retrieval of (self-validating) past moments, seems an instinctual aspect of national identity. This book considers how these literary works are received and *put to work* in the present. The 'sceptr'd Isle' speech is quoted because people believe it communicates something timeless about England – admittedly by taking the reader back to a 'golden age' – but one that is pertinent for us, here and now. The 'sceptr'd Isle' naturalizes its depiction of England on various levels. 'This fortress built by Nature for herself' grounds Englishness in an empirical stability (while not an island, it is nonetheless believed to be constituted by its coastline and boundaries).[58] Gaunt's speech is believed to express a truth about England that Shakespeare – in his quintessential English genius – perfectly articulated.

Although a linguistic and aesthetic phenomenon, literature becomes an event in reading, an act between an individual and a text.

It is the contention of this book that it is in the act of reading – an act that 'performs' and as such iterates discursive and aesthetic constructions of Englishness – that national identity is linked, in its everyday activities, to its heritage. In reading the liturgy at the heart of *The Secret Garden*, Protestant convictions are potentially revived in the reader. This book considers the literature of the past – the poetry of Spenser, Milton and then William Wordsworth and the prose of George Eliot, Thomas Hardy and George Orwell – for how it articulates and circumscribes a Protestant logic in an aesthetic register and helps to establish and continue a mythology of English simplicity.

MYTHOLOGIES

In calling simplicity a 'Protestant aesthetic', I am drawing attention to its formal properties and consider these in the light of Roland Barthes' theories of mythology. Like the term 'aesthetic', 'mythology' refers to something's form not its content. Myths are not, then, stories now known not to be true – *mythos* (imagination) as opposed to *logos* (reasoning).[59] In semiological terms, Barthes presents myth as a '*second-order semiological system*' (*Mythologies,* p. 137), a sign in which an arbitrary relation between signifier and signified is presented as natural – for example the relation between simplicity and honesty. In Barthes' terms, myth 'speaks', it is motivated, 'it points out and it notifies, it makes us understand something and it imposes it on us' (p. 140). Myth is motivated in the sense that it asserts a position without redress to evidence or argument: simplicity *is* honesty. The sign speaks clearly, then, of the property or concept it signifies, but it disguises the historical or constructed nature of the link. Barthes' description of myth as a '*second-order semiological system*' gives a spatial metaphor to the semiotic process – that he concedes is 'only a metaphor' (p. 137) – of a surface-level order which is also at the same time a second-level order. The surface meaning 'is *already* complete, it postulates a kind of knowledge, a past, a memory, a comparative order of facts, ideas, decisions' (p. 141). This surface 'does not suppress the meaning, it only impoverishes it, it puts it at a distance, it holds it at one's disposal' (p. 141). Importantly, Barthes explains, 'the very end of myths is to immobilize the world' (p. 183), in other words, myths 'mimic a universal order' that suspends the realities of life behind a screen of appealing cleanness: 'it abolishes the complexity of human acts, it gives them the simplicity of essences', 'it organizes a world without contradictions because it is without depth' (p. 170). Simplicity in many ways is an exemplary myth, which works by presenting what in reality is complex, messy and heterogeneous, in a singular (or simple) form: what could be more obvious than the fact that simplicity must be simple? History, cultural background, fissures and contradictions are overwhelmed and masked by a form that is seductively straightforward and, importantly, that appears natural. So, the specifically historical dimension to simplicity's association with the theological (hermeneutic transparency), the moral (honesty, integrity) and the rational (singular lines of logic, superior discernment) is held at a distance, leaving a straightforward sign of simplicity as a signifier of transparency, honesty, integrity, logic and discernment.

A key element of Barthes' outline of mythology, then, is its disguising of the historical. Simplicity's seemingly natural signifying of transparency obscures the historical construct of Protestant concepts about hermeneutic transparency. The political possibilities of presenting the historical and contingent as natural are articulated as far back as Plato's advocation of a state mythology that produces subjects who act according to habit. This process is described by Littlejohns and Soncini as a 'strategy of occult persuasion grounded on repetition'.[60] They claim in their excellent analysis of myth that this metamorphosis from complex historical to simple nature is a reversible formula: 'there is always a possibility of restoring that story to its original complexity, fragmentariness and contradiction by bringing to light its different, competing versions' (p. 18).[61] This belief in the restoration of complexity is one premise upon which this book is based: that simplicity can be revealed to be not so simple. And yet Barthes insists that the reversal process is not so easy, and it is his demonstration of mythology's tenacity that explains simplicity's long legacy. He demonstrates that what makes mythology so resilient is its resistance to any revelations of its 'true' nature. He explains that *myth hides nothing*: its function is to distort, not to make disappear' (p. 145). As Manfred Pfister eloquently explains, 'One important task that myths perform is to prevent questions, to forestall their being asked in the first place.'[62] Barthes explains that

> myth essentially aims at causing an immediate impression – it does not matter if one is later allowed to see through the myth, its

action is assumed to be stronger than the rational explanations which may later belie it. This means that the reading of myth is exhausted at one stroke.

He goes on: 'A more attentive reading of the myth will in no way increase its power or its effectiveness: a myth is at the same time imperfectible and unquestionable; time or knowledge will not make it better or worse' (p. 155). As such, and as will be argued in this book, simplicity's association with transparency and honesty – even when the relation is revealed as historically contingent, arbitrary and artificial – is difficult to disentwine.

Myths are convincing and resilient, then, precisely because they rise above the flux and intricacy of everyday life; instead they present formulas that correspond to elements of reality (and are, as such, convincing) in such a way as to render it easier to grasp. Mythology may or not be 'true' when considered empirically, but it still retains an aura of believability. Indeed, it takes little effort to show how the English are not simple: early industrialization and urbanization challenges the image of a green and pleasant land. Myth, in fact, invites a suspension of belief as it aims to disable cognitive engagement and instead sets itself up as too harmless, as too appealing, to provoke dissent or interrogation.

AESTHETICS AND DISPOSITIONS

How does Englishness, as composed of apparently elusive yet 'recognizable' elements (such as simplicity) endure and contain such emotional hold on individuals? If there is no script or dogma, how are ideas or attitudes passed on and recognized so easily? Englishness depends upon both the visceral, emotional realm and the aesthetic register for its resilience. What is important is not just the ways that aesthetics and their related bodily acts and impulses impel us, but also how they implicate the world that we act within: that dispositions produce objects in their own image, and vice versa. As such, I follow Judith Butler (among others), although turn the focus away from sexual and gendered bodies to other aspects of our identity, namely national identities (although all of these facets are always imbricated). That an individual is never purely rational is in many ways old news; the non-rational is foregrounded in Freud's emphasis upon unconscious impulses and by Foucault's emphasis upon the power of society and regimes of knowledge to regulate the body and mind. What I hope to show in this book is the ways in which aesthetics and ritual (the actions of our bodies) function on a non-rational register and have power to shape and influence the rational mind.

A specific aesthetic (such as simplicity) implicates the individual because an aesthetic, and especially such a morally constituted one, has taste as its counterpart. In Kantian or phenomenological terms this may well merely suggest the relation of the exterior world as experienced, and constructed, through the senses. In Bourdieuian terms, an aesthetic such as simplicity necessitates a disposition in the perceiver – in this case a discernment of the superiority of the simple. The two are necessarily complementary. The continuation of an aesthetic, then, means the continuation of its corresponding disposition. When Addison, Johnson or Wordsworth assert the superiority of simplicity they are reflecting, as well as encouraging, a preference for the simple in their readers. An aesthetic reflects the practices of the apparently natural preferences of everyday life – of simple lines over the ornate and the glistering. The two, the aesthetic and the disposition, are therefore mutually constitutive – an expression of the superiority of a text's simplicity reflects a belief in the superiority of simplicity in that text's authors and readers.

Louis Althusser and Pierre Bourdieu both have as their object of study the practices of the everyday; and yet both of these theorists are concerned with the ways in which the past is imprinted on the present, or rather how it is habitually passed on, with the heritage of the past as lived out in ritual practice. I want to expand – or rather elaborate – their writing on ritual and apply it to the aesthetic – not a difficult move as a disposition is always motivated towards an object, an object that consequently becomes endowed with an auratic quality. Both Althusser and Boudieu take inspiration from Pascal's *Pensées*. Althusser outlines the importance of this 'wonderful formula',

> which will enable us to invert the order of the notional schema of ideology. Pascal says more or less: 'Kneel down, move your lips in prayer, and you will believe.' He thus scandalously inverts the order of things [ ][63]

Both take from Pascal, then, this 'scandalous' inversion of the intuitive order of things; moving from a rationalist and mind-centred trajectory in which decision leads to belief to a bodily-centred trajectory in which it is action ('kneel down') that leads to faith.

Althusser's writings further demonstrate the ways in which the individual freely consents to act and freely partakes of the rituals of everyday activity that work to materialize beliefs within her everyday life (corresponding to Butlerian theories of performativity). Whereas Althusser's Marxist emphasis leads him to trace the motivation behind individual activity to the state (and to 'Ideological State Apparatuses' such as schools and government), Bourdieu writes more specifically about the individual's take-up of ritual activity from his surrounding culture. He writes:

> Rites are practices that are ends in themselves, that are justified by their very performance; things that are done because they are 'the done thing', 'the right thing to do', but also because one cannot do otherwise, without needing to know why or for whom one does them, or what they mean, such as acts of funeral piety.[64]

As such, Bourdieu recognizes the intuitively common sense nature of the rituals that individuals partake in and their inherently social nature. They are not only 'the done thing', but deviation from them necessitates explanation. No reasons are needed to comply, yet reasons must be given to differ. He goes on to explain it as 'behaviour that is both "sensible" and devoid of sense intention' (p. 18), in other words, that appears as reasonable but that is devoid of explicit reasoning. Behaviour is 'a symbolism that is neither entirely logical nor entirely illogical, neither entirely controlled nor entirely unconscious' (p. 20), and as such cannot be attenuated into the conscious, rational and decision-making individual on the one hand or to non-conscious activities on the other. Both play a crucial part in constructing identity. Like Althusser, Bourdieu traces his conviction back to a reading of Pascal and namely his assertion that: 'Proofs only convince the mind; habit provides the strongest proofs and those that are most believed [. . .] It is, then, habit that convinces us and makes so many Christians' (p. 48). He extrapolates elements of Pascal's emphasis on habit in order to produce his theory of *habitus*, and expounds in the following passage how this helps to explain the relation between past and present, between heritage and present activity, that this present study of Englishness is indebted to:

> The *habitus*, a product of history, produces individual and collective practices – more history – in accordance with the schemes

generated by history. It ensures the active presence of past experiences, which, deposited in each organism in the form of schemes of perception, thought and action, tend to guarantee the 'correctness' of practices and their constancy over time, more reliably than all formal rules and explicit norms. This system of dispositions – a present past that tends to perpetuate itself into the future by reactivation in similarly structured practices, an internal law through which the law of external necessities, irreducible to immediate constraints, is constantly exerted – is the principle of the continuity and regularity which objectivism sees in social practices without being able to account for it; and also of the regulated transformations that cannot be explained either by the extrinsic, instantaneous determinations of mechanistic sociologism or by the purely internal but equally instantaneous determination of spontaneist subjectivism. (p. 54)

Bourdieu is responding explicitly to the problem of theorists' identification of 'continuity and regularity' that they are not 'able to account for'. Bourdieu suggests that practices construct an 'internal law' that becomes the lens through which the world is experienced. The past becomes an 'active present' through a set of 'dispositions', a term Bourdieu uses to sum up the whole set of 'schemes of perception, thought and action' that he sees as the more efficient vehicle of the past than concepts or regulations. He sees these dispositions as guaranteeing a degree of continuity. Agency is shaped not by either external motivations (the effect of outside pressures) or the impulses of the individual, but necessarily a messy mixture of both that results in the 'regulated transformations' of repetition and alterity.

The relation between disposition, nature and habit is frequently engaged with, to different degrees, and with different levels of acknowledgement, by writers included in this book. Joseph Addison, who will feature in Chapter Two, engages with the workings of disposition in *The Spectator*. Here, Addison insists on the relation between taste in writing and the olfactory, asserting that the faculty of 'taste', 'must in some degree be born with us', pushing the limits of 'in some degree' in his assertion of the construction of taste, so that the reading of 'fine writing' produces a reader who 'naturally wears himself into the same manner of speaking and thinking', 'naturally' indicating here causality rather than essence.[65] His recourse to nature is undermined by his assertion that custom 'is able to form a

man anew, and to give him inclinations and capacities altogether different from those he was born with'.[66] Addison indicates an almost
evangelical process of rebirth. He goes on to explain: 'The mind
grows fond of those actions she is accustomed to, and is drawn with
reluctancy from those paths in which she has been used to walk'
(p. 277). He draws the conclusion that a man engaged in activities
through others' choice or necessity, although finding it 'disagreeable
to him at first', with 'use and application will certainly render it not
only less painful, but pleasing and satisfactory' (p. 278). In quoting
Pythagoras's aphorism – 'Pitch upon that course of life which is the
most excellent and custom will render it the most delightful' – he
posits reason's superiority to inclination: 'inclination will at length
come over to reason, though we can never force reason to comply
with inclination' (p. 279). In other words: do the rational thing and
feeling will follow. But he also suggests the opposite: bodily acts will
impel a new mindset. He goes on to warn his readers: 'we must, in
this world, gain a relish of truth and virtue, if we would be able to
taste that knowledge and perfection, which are to make us happy in
the next' (p. 280). A taste for truth, virtue and heaven must be cultivated, in other words: 'heaven is not to be looked upon only as the
reward, but as the natural effect, of a religious life' (p. 281). The distinction between action and decision is slippery: custom is located
outside the body and mind, effecting both, a separation that compli-
cates the relation between action and decision. He wishes to separate
the natural and the cultivated but his attempts serve only to illustrate
their messy overlap.

The body as the vehicle of transition between the past and present
is also explored in George Eliot's preface to *Middlemarch* (a text also
explored in Chapter Two). She calls up the life of Theresa which is
often read as a frame for the protagonist, Dorothea, giving her a
saintly trajectory. The passage explicitly sets itself up as answering
questions of the 'history of man, and how the mysterious mixture
behaves under the varying experiments of Time'. She looks to the
young Theresa and her 'still smaller brother', setting out to 'seek
martyrdom in the country of the Moors'. She notes their 'human
hearts, already beating to a national idea', the pulse of the heart suggesting an image of an irresistible musical rhythm to which new
recruits cannot help but come into step with. Eliot's purpose is to
dwell on the historical structures that constrain women's activities,
but in doing so she emphasizes the relation between the individual

and the nation, a nation painted in terms of a rhythm to which each new life joins. This beating echoes with Bourdieu's 'dispositions' to suggest a visceral core to heritage and continuation. Eliot's disparaging of the Tullivers in *The Mill on the Floss*, that they 'seem to have no standard beyond hereditary custom', has a positive counterpart in Tom and Maggie who are tied to 'the mental level of the generation before them' by 'the strongest fibres of their hearts'.[67] Hereditary custom untempered by thought is juxtaposed with the emotional ties of inherited attitudes demonstrating its potentially negative or positive, yet pervasive, influence upon the individual.

As human beings we are implicated in our activities. We are conditioned as much by what we do as what we decide and choose; and even choice itself cannot be located solely in an autonomous individual. Bodily acts create dispositions, preferences, which in turn create a moral sphere within which we view the material world. And, conversely, valorized objects create preferences that in turn impel specific bodily behaviour. This book looks partly, then, at what Englishness means in the body and how we react to other bodies: what they wear, what they do, how they act. We judge others' clothes and bodies morally, but often not by ethical but aesthetic criteria. The way a person stands, although not an ethical action in and of itself, is considered morally: standing upright or slouching is read as significant. We take the aesthetic, the visual, the bodily, and we frame it in moral terms. Why is this so? In England at least, a partial answer is that the Protestantism of the Reformation took over the whole of life: the whole of the material, natural and human world is implicated in the divine scheme.

Chapter One outlines the precise set of Protestant beliefs that were invested in simplicity: both anti-Catholic rejection of ostentation and hermeneutical assumptions of transparency. Through readings of Edmund Spenser's *The Faerie Queene* and John Milton's *Paradise Lost*, simplicity is shown to be a key signifier that is the conceptual foundation to other characteristics of Englishness, namely rationality, self-control, and freedom. Simplicity becomes, in these works, a marker of the elect English. The continuance of the aesthetic of simplicity into eighteenth- and nineteenth-century literature, and its ongoing dependence upon an unarticulated belief in transparency, is considered in Chapter Two. Here, simplicity is shown to morph from a theologically infused concept to one that comes to be an intuitive value that itself measures theological and moral positions. The theologically informed oppositional force of simplicity persists and it becomes a more general (rather than theologically specific) arbitrator of morality and a marker of the elite. Chapter Three continues the trajectory to twentieth- and twenty-first-century writings on Englishness, demonstrating how contemporary accounts of a nostalgic Englishness are dependent upon the literary depiction of a simple Englishness based in the landscape, an Englishness that is still oppositional and in which simplicity acts as a marker of pre-eminence. This chapter also demonstrates the importance of those character traits that are indebted to simplicity (as revealed in Chapter One): rationality, discernment, self-possession, reservation and self-control. The final chapter turns to a specific outworking of the oppositional force of the Protestant aesthetic of English simplicity that is apparent in articulations of Islamophobia.

With the book covering such a large scope – the subjects of Englishness, of simplicity and of Islamophobia, as well as an immense period from the early modern to the present day, there is necessarily a sense of speed to the book. I have no doubt that others are more suited to write different sections of this book and that they can be fleshed out with more nuance and therefore with greater panache than I have managed. These chapters are intended to sketch out the persistence of simplicity, and the ways in which its Protestant logics of transparency and supremacy are in force in contemporary expressions of Englishness and especially implicated in Islamophobia.

CHAPTER ONE

THE ENGLISH REFORMATION AND THE PROTESTANT AESTHETIC

> *But all the doctrine, which he taught and gave,*
> *Was cleare as heav'n, from whence it came.*
> *At least those beams of truth, which onley save,*
> *Surpasse in brightness any flame.*
>   *from George Herbert, 'Divinitie', ll. 13–16.*

Herbert's image of doctrine as 'cleare as heav'n' suggests a celestial purity and brilliance that persists despite his 'At least', a qualification that narrows his assertion to saving doctrines only, following the emphasis of Reformed theologians. That it is only certain doctrines that are defended as transparent, as superlatively bright, does little to taint the overriding image that persists in Herbert's stanza of the transferral of heaven to earth, of doctrine's clarity, purity, truth and life. It is in poetic form that Reformation doctrines elide technical qualifications to instil in the reader a lasting impression of the intimacy of divine truth for the Protestant individual. This chapter considers the construction of English simplicity in the early modern period and how it came to signify Protestant access to truth, honesty, discernment and self-control.

Edmund Spenser's *The Faerie Queene*, though far from a simple tale, constructs simplicity as a cornerstone aesthetic. The epic poem narrates England and Protestantism through an allegory of knights fighting for their faerie queene in faerieland. It opens, in its first book, on the Redcrosse knight, the first book being, as John King has argued in relation to idolatry, paradigmatic of the whole work.[1] Idolatry (Latin, *eidola*, things seen) is an essentially aesthetic theology that makes book I equally paradigmatic of Spenser's wider aesthetics and it will be the primary focus of my discussion here. The knight's red cross emblem on his shield, from which he takes his name, fuses the St. George cross and the Protestant crucifix. The cross is described as the 'remembrance of his dying lord', the term 'remembrance' invoking the Protestant emphasis on the eucharist as sign not real presence. The red cross, then, symbolizes the knight's quest as both a specifically Protestant journey of redemption and the Englishman's journey to self-actualization. It is an imbrication underlined by Spenser's use of Arthurian legend that colours his whole epic in national terms.

From its very beginning, Spenser's epic demands a familiarly Protestant Scriptural mode of reading. His expressed and often cited purpose for the poem is to 'fashion a gentleman' ('Letter to Raleigh', p. 714), and in the first book it is apparent that part of this fashioning is to construct a more attentive reader. The glorious knight is 'in mightie armes and siluer shielde' that bear the 'cruell markes of many a bloody fielde', even though 'Yet armes till that time did he neuer wield' (I. i. 1). The curious mixture of the legacy of battle in his battered armour and the knight's inexperience is made understandable only through recourse to the biblical text of Ephesians 6. If the 'siluer shielde' is to be understood as the shield of faith, then the knight is rightly a novice, taking on the armour of God in his inheritance of the Christian journey. Through the saturation of his poem in biblical imagery, Spenser encourages, or more accurately necessitates, the reader's propensity to refer back to the Bible in all interpretive effort. The Bible becomes *The Faerie Queene*'s parallel text as it does in so many other early modern works; through repeated and detailed reference to the Bible, the reader's task is set out as that of interpretation through a biblical code, so that he or she can only decipher the text by use of a biblical lens.

Spenser's poem draws heavily on John Bale's commentary on Revelation, *The Image of Both Churches* (1545), which presents allegorically polarized female figures recognizable in Spenser as Una (the one, true church) and Duessa (duplicitous Catholicism). Bale's commentary demonstrates the degree to which many articulations of Protestantism highlighted the importance of perception in its attention to the Christian's own discernment of the true from the false church through biblical interpretation.[2] This Reformation emphasis upon discrimination is vital to the knight's success. Although setting off on an explicitly Christian quest (with the red cross and carrying biblical armour), it soon becomes clear that Redcrosse is not a good reader – he encounters clear signs of evil and is ignorant to their warnings. It is these misreadings that provoke the reader to a self-reflexivity about interpretation, that David Norbrook has called 'alienation effects', which warn the reader away from taking 'interpretations they are offered in trust'.[3]

Spenser destabilizes signification in the opening stanza of book I as we are introduced simultaneously, and rather paradoxically, to the stable sign of the red cross and to the problematic signifier 'seem'd'. The knight himself is indubitably a reliable Protestant sign. The guarantee of meaning in his 'bloodie Crosse' is underlined in book II when the knight Guyon mistakenly charges Redcrosse, thinking him the perpetrator of evil deeds, but he pulls up when he is assured by the sign of the red cross:

> And with reprochfull shame mine honour shent,
> Whilse cursed steele against that badge I bent,
> The sacred badge of my Redeemer's death,
> Which on your shield is set for ornament.

Here, as Guyon charges to slay Redcrosse, it is the 'ornament' of the red cross that shames him of his accusatory attack and convinces him of Redcrosse's virtue. That the red cross is only a stable sign for those of redeemed sight is evident in Sans Foy's misconstrual (see Chapter Four, p. 101).

Although stabilized by his red cross, the knight in the first stanza is one who jolly 'seem'd', a term that posits semblance (this is what he looked like) but plays with the ontological uncertainty of appearance (this is not necessarily, however, what he *is*). Flagged so early on, the word 'seem'd' is a warning to the reader throughout the poem, a warning that is later warranted in the deceptive looks of Archimago and Duessa and that is used repeatedly as a marker of dishonesty (the magician Archimago's duplicity is contrasted with Una's sincerity with the phrase 'th'enchaunter ioyous seemde no less', I. iii. 32). What is seen, the poet suggests, is the surface that offers no guarantee of the substance. The symbols and signs that are seen by the knight himself certainly are not self-evident enough to guarantee understanding. Indeed, Redcrosse is a reliable misinterpreter of sur-faces who is led astray by his enemies.

How can Spenser present a solid sign (the red cross) while ques-tioning signification? Spenser is demanding an alert readership: his assertion of the necessity of discernment needs a world of lethally untrustworthy signs. What he is drawing his reader's attention to is that signs are only reliable for the reformed individual. *The Faerie Queene* as a text performs a hermeneutical lesson, familiar to Calvin-influenced England in which Word, world and self were signs to be read (see p. 35). Despite his recognition of the complexity of inter-pretation, Spenser nonetheless asserts true representation. As the 'bloodie crosse' is a reliable signifier of the reformed individual, so Una, the representative of the one true Church (Protestantism) 'did seem such, as she was' in her 'self-resemblance' (I. xii. 8) (just as Duessa claims 'I that do seeme not I', I. v. 26). Both the cross and Una present Spenser's ideal: that the thing is as it appears, the sign is a reliable indicator of reality. 'Una' emphasizes simplicity: of the church and doctrine which leads logically to singularity of interpret-ation. Even though *The Faerie Queene* reveals, again and again, the impossibility of transparency, the aesthetic of simplicity nonetheless communicates an unproblematic hermeneutic of plain reading in a form potentially more convincing (and less subject to rational contra-diction) than a theological treatise.

The durability of simplicity's transparency is illustrated by his depiction of the three graces in book VI (which themselves indicate the qualities of divine grace, the pinnacle of Reformed theology). Here we find the repetition of the questionable signifier 'seem' (which refers to smiling and forward position), whereas they 'are' naked:

> Therefore they always smoothly seem to smile,
>> That we likewise should mild and gentle be,
>> And also naked are, that without guile
>> Or false dissemblance all them plain may see,
>> Simple and true from covert malice free:
>> And eek them selves so in their dance they bore,
>> That two of them still forward seemed to be.
>> But one still towards showed her self afore:
> That good should from us go, then come in greater store. (VI. x. 24)

Their nakedness is a sign of their truth and lack of malicious pretence ('guile'), a stable signifier of their internal state. The warning inherent in 'seen' threatens the assertion of plain reading, yet the disclosure of transparency's impossibility does not render simplicity's myth less compelling. As Barthes has argued, mythology's 'function is to distort, not to make disappear' ('Myth Today', p. 145) and 'myth is neither a lie nor a confession: it is an inflexion' (p. 153). As the removal of form, nudity intuitively signifies access. '[A]ll them plain may see' works on the assumption of nudity's openness to assert a mind free from hidden motivation, 'covert malice'. That we are reminded that smiles ('seem to smile') and even perspective ('forward seemed', in the *trompe l'oeil* for example) can be deceptive does nothing to undermine the guarantee assumed in nakedness's exterior form. That which is intuited – literally apprehended by immediate perception – is also naturalized and resistant to rational contradiction. To repeat Barthes' assertion of myth's power: 'A more attentive reading of the myth will in no way increase its power or its ineffectiveness' (p. 155).

Access to naked truth is dependent upon redeemed sight. Redcrosse becomes a good reader only when he is taken to the House of Holiness and taught to read by the character Fidelia (faith). The knight is introduced by Fidelia to 'a booke that was both signd and seald with blood/ Wherein darke things were writt, hard to be vnderstood' (1. 10. 13), describing for Spenser's readers the Christian Scriptures. The phrase 'darke things were writt' signals most obviously the book's opacity.[4] Like *The Faerie Queene* – itself labelled a 'darke conceit' by Spenser – it eludes immediate or easy comprehension.[5] Fidelia, rather than merely passing on an indecipherable document, helpfully also bestows the ability to interpret, for 'none could reade, except she did them teach'. The book's darkness is specific, then, to the uninitiated, as Calvin writes: 'in the simplicitie which is seen in the Gospell, there is such wisdome of God as is incomprensible vnlesse it please him to reuele it too vs by his holie spirit' (*Ephesians*, pp. 342–3). Fidelia 'vnto him disclosed euery whitt' suggests a profound change in Redcrosse's perception. With faith, Fidelia, Redcrosse can understand everything including 'Of God, of grace, of iustice, of free will', a fine Protestant nexus of complex doctrines. For the redeemed reader, even the 'darke' book of Revelation is perspicuous. Scriptural knowledge becomes, in Calvin's terms, like spectacles that bestow superior sight:

For as olde men, or poore blind, or they whose eies ar dimme sighted, if you lay a faire boke before them, though they perceiue that there is somewhat written therin, yet can they not reade two words together: but being holpen with spectacles set betwen them and it, they begin to reade distinctlye: so the Scripture gathering vp together in our mindes the knowledge of God, whiche otherwise is but confused, doeth remoue the mist, and plainly shewe vs the true god. This therefore is a singular gifte, that to the instruccion of his church God vseth not onely dumme teachers, but also openeth his owne holye mouth[.] (*Inst,* 1.6)

Fidelia bestows a superlative level of perception meaning that Redcrosse has a redeemed interpretive ability. Bale's *The Image of Both Churches,* so hugely influential upon Spenser's allegory, presents in unequivocal terms the Protestant belief in signs that are stable for elect readers but mysterious to the reprobate. Of the untrue church, Babylon, the outward indicates internal qualities, 'Her verye name agreynge to her frutes' (p. 127). As such: 'Thys is to the faythfull sort/ as a written name of her/ euydent/ clere open and manyfest. But to the vnfaythfull yt ys onlye as a mysterye/ hidden/ darke/ obscure/ and neglect.' The Protestant aesthetic is counter-intuitive, for 'the secretes that God openeth to babes' he 'hydeth from the wyse'. In short, it is a belief in perspicuity for the elect or redeemed: the Scriptures are transparent to render God's Word and will as they 'doeth remove the mist'. This new redeemed sight is evident in Bunyan's *The Pilgrim's Progress,* in which Luxon identifies, in his *Literal Figures: Puritan Allegory and the Reformation Crisis in Representation,* an outworking of Protestant hermeneutics. The unredeemed 'mistake types and shadows, figures and similitudes, all the things of "this World," including themselves, for what is real' whereas those 'born again, who have experienced the true birth of which birth into this world is a mere shadowy figure, walk through this world as if walking through an allegory, just as Christian, Faithful, and Hopeful walk through the landscape of *The Pilgrim's Progress*' (p. 159). Reading is only straightforward, then, for those who have the code to decipher the world. Redeemed sight extends to the world in which God is manifest, as Calvin insists, God 'to wrappe al mankind in one giltinesse, doeth shewe his diuine maiestie to al withoute excepcion as it wer portraied out in his creatures' (*Inst,* 1.6). What Calvin, Bale, Bunyan and Spenser assert is a whole new level of perspicuity.

Superior Protestant interpretive ability, and its relation to simplicity, is proven at Redcrosse's betrothal to his beloved Una at the end of the book. Here he is accosted by the enchanter Archimago, who in disguise brings a letter from the 'false Duessa' to disrupt the marriage. Redcrosse draws attention to Duessa's duplicity and goes on to explain that her surface appearance finds easy prey in those of weak sight, referring back to his former, unredeemed self:

> Most false *Duessa*, royall richly dight,
> That easy was t'inueigle weaker sight:
> Who by her wicked arts, and wiely skill,
> Too false and strong for earthly skill or might[.] (I. xii. 32)

The stanza qualifies 'weaker sight' with 'earthly skill or might', suggesting heavenly vision as the safeguard against deception. His betrothed, Una (who, as the one true Church of Protestantism is also an emblem of Reformation interpretive ability), reveals the innocent-looking messenger to be none other than the enchanter Archimago. His evil nature in this scene is masked with the very sign of truthfulness: 'this false footman, clokt with simpleness' (I. xii. 34), a guise that for Una makes him the 'falsest man alive'. Falseness inevitably masks itself with declarations of truth, indeed the letter received earlier in this scene has the deceptive Duessa plead disingenuously in her defence: 'For truth is strong, her rightfull cause to plead' (I. xii. 28). The appropriate disguise for duplicity, then, is its opposite 'simpleness'. That the aesthetic of simplicity coincides with a belief in transparency is evident in the next line in which Una beseeches her listeners that

> if ye please for to discouer plaine,
> Ye shall *Archimago* find.

To 'discover plaine' is to dis-cover, or uncover, the guise identified as plain, simplicity; but to 'discover plaine' is also to reveal truth: beneath simplicity-as-disguise, there is still, nonetheless, the 'plain' truth. The word and world may be full of 'darke things', but they are 'plain' to those of redeemed sight.

Whereas Catholics were accused of mistaking the sign for the thing signified in their veneration of bread and wine, Protestants instead took possession of the world as a set of signs to which they had privileged access. At the Reformation, a visceral act of salvation (eating the actual body) became a ritual of signification; the act became a memorial, pointing beyond the ritual itself to the belief of the individual, and through that belief, to an internalized sense of salvation that worked through personal response. What was once an act, something material, became semiological. And in this way the material world too entered the realm of semiology – everything was sign. Of course, that the world became semiological heralded a multiplication of interpretations but it had little effect on individuals' claims to perfect explanation. Of course, the world had for a long time been a signifier of God's will: there was not much new in seeing God's displeasure in disasters, or his pleasure in political triumphs. But what people learnt from reading the complex and metaphorical language of the Bible (in which Jesus is both gate and bread) is that things were never what they seemed. Everything was significant not just of itself, but of a higher reality and a more profound truth. Such suspicion about appearances may seem to contradict claims about the transparency of Scripture. But the world's transparency depends on a sanctified reader, on Calvin's 'spectacles'. Selective transparency depends on a coded world only decipherable by the chosen few.

As a set of surfaces the world was not 'true' reality. But the world-as-surface, if properly read, would reveal the deeper, more profound, divine 'reality'. As Luxon explains, Reformation principles of reading rendered 'the past as an allegory of the present and the present as an allegory of the future' (p. 26). In other words, the material world (including history) signified a greater spiritual reality – and the present was only ever a signifier of the greater truth of the future fulfilment of God's will. The only reality was one that pertained to God, and as such the material surfaces of the world were never significant in and of themselves. The material was never separate from the spiritual: it signified, it too spoke of God (in the way that Milton's Satan, despite his best efforts, works within the pre-ordained will of God). Practices of reading Scripture and eucharist cascaded out to the mundanity of everyday life. In the early autobiography of Rose Thurgood, written in 1636–7, her narrative presents her as an interpreter of the signs of her life. Before conversion she is a bad interpreter and infers from the facts of her impoverished life her own reprobation; after conversion she asserts her clarity of sight, so that where her poverty had previously signified God's judgement, she now reads in it an economy of divine preference for the humble.[6]

Even before the waning of religious belief, it is evident that in literature of the early modern period that semiology quickly becomes mythology: the world continues to be semiotic, it is ubiquitously significant, but the values signified have become so imbued within their signifiers that they are indistinguishable. Complex systems of theological significance soon became a set of shorthand signs. Whereas for the Reformers simple Scripture was only revelatory and brought salvation to those who had the aid of the Holy Spirit, simplicity came more straightforwardly to signify transparency. Even on the level of morality, the sign of simplicity-as-honesty is arbitrary: it is the contingent turned natural. The pared down aesthetics of simplicity are a signifier of God's imbuing of vision that gives the individual sight. This equation is rendered mythological when the middle stage is removed: simplicity becomes a signifier of immediate intuition. What was once dependent upon a complex understanding of God's grace becomes a passive engagement with the world in which signifiers are mistaken for signs – in other words, what is perceived is not simplicity in and of itself (which may, indeed, be a negative quality that signifies stupidity or lack of complexity) but moral virtue: the signified of honesty has become indistinguishable from the signifier of simplicity.

Transparency becomes coupled with the aesthetic of simplicity (exemplified in plain reading, but also plain clothes, simple rurality and the simple life) and signifies a wealth of interconnected qualities. As was implicit in *The Faerie Queene*, simplicity signifies rationalism in the elect's newly superior discerning mind. The emphasis upon Protestant discernment leads to a widespread association of God-given perception with a God-given reason. Philip Sidney states a hierarchy between the 'erected wit' and the 'infected will', the rational former recognizing 'what perfection is', while the latter 'keepth us from reaching unto it'.[7] While acknowledging humanity's Fall from grace, what Calvinists would call human depravity, Protestants repeatedly construct the individual as essentially reasoning. The Protestant conversion narrative, although finding its foundation in Calvinist predestination that apparently posits God as driving force, seemingly undermining the individual's agency, is nonetheless dependent upon a moment of articulated assent to Christ's sovereignty. And we see that Redcrosse is rationally controlled and self-possessed after his stay at the House of Holiness, where before he had been rash and hasty. After he receives redeemed sight, he gains control over himself and grows quickly to 'such perfection of heuenly grace' (I. xii. 21) until in stanza 45 'so perfect he became' that he learns a superlative level of moral goodness: 'His mortall life he learned had to frame/ In holy righteousnesse, without rebuke or blame.' Righteousness is a result of self-framing, an interpretative response to the self which is a heightened understanding and form of self-control that enables amelioration.

The Faerie Queene exposes simplicity's relation to personal self-control. As the eschewing of ornament or luxury, simplicity represents a self-possession that is perhaps one of the most historically resilient characteristics of mythic Englishness. In book II, canto vii, the knight Guyon can eschew ornament, enacted in his resistance of the material lure of Mammon. Because he is temperate (his humours are perfectly balanced), he can control the mixture of impulses in his body. Mammon represents not merely wealth, but the ornateness of Catholicism; his

> [. . .] cote all overgrowne with rust,
> Was vnderneath enueloped with gold,
> Whose glistering glosse darkned with filthy dust,
> Well yet appeared, to haue been of old
> A worke of rich entayle, and curious mould,
> Wouen with antickes and wyld imagery[.] (vii. 4)

As revealed in Ignaro's rusty keys in I.viii.30 (see discussion on p. 38), rust indicates disuse, and Mammon's 'glistering gloss', his 'curious mould' (elaborately wrought design), his 'antickes' (fantastic figures) and 'wyld imagery' are all of no purpose, merely vacuous excess.

For the Protestant aesthetic, then, truthfulness, rationalism and self-control are intertwined and resultant from the theology of transparency communicated in simplicity. That this trajectory is one that elides difficulties and complexities is perhaps all-too-apparent: these are mythologies that elide, not refer to, the world. As an aesthetic, simplicity succeeds in suppressing 'orthodoxy's own suppressed contradictions', as Luxon has called them (*Literal Figures*, p. 6). That simplicity's rich signification is not always consciously identified is apparent in Crispin Sartwell's definition of Reformation and modern-day American Shaker aesthetics as 'sublime in their simplicity, clear in their usefulness, perfect in their craft, an apotheosis resting on humility' (p. 205). While noting the sublimity, clarity and perfection that simplicity invokes, as well as its heuristic application ('an apotheosis'), he nonetheless rather narrowly identifies humility as the foundational signified of simplicity (its key signification before the Reformation in England).

Simplicity in Spenser is always an oppositional quality: it takes its meaning not primarily from the complexity that it masks, but its aesthetic counterparts, ostentation and opacity and their related moral qualities of dishonesty and error.[8] Such anti-Catholic oppositional logic is presented by Spenser as a specifically English quality. Redcrosse is, after all later identified as St. George and he carries the English standard. Spenser reminds the reader of simplicity's relation to Englishness in his description of the respective ushers to two houses Redcrosse encounters: the evil House of Pride (whose usher is the resplendent Vanitie) and the House of Holiness (with the 'sober' Reverence). The usher is the person who represents the house to the outside world, who leads the person into the heart of the home. In the House of Pride and in Redcrosse's encounter with the giant Orgoglio, we are introduced to the important symbolic role of the usher or porter. Named Ignaro, Orgoglio's porter presents an aesthetic of ignorance symbolized in the keys for the inner doors, which 'unused rust did overgrowe' (I. viii. 30). The rusted keys indicate that ignorance has no means to enter, and thereby know or explore, interiority. If we follow King in applying the Geneva Bible's interpretation of the keys of heaven in Matthew 16.19 as 'the worde of God' (*Spenser's Poetics*, p. 100) then Ignaro likewise has no access to the truth that the Scriptures hold. As such, interiority and biblical interpretation are implicated in each other. The righteous Prince Arthur, in contrast, takes hold of the keys and easily gains access to the whole of the castle (I. viii. 34). In King's analysis Ignaro is compared to the House of Holiness's Contemplation and Fidelia, who together 'represent the moral opposite of Ignaro as personifications of the introspective faith and knowledge fostered by scriptural understanding (I. x. 50)' (p. 99). King's emphasis is on interiority, but Spenser articulates an externally rendered moral world, for example in the image of keys. In formal terms the counterparts of Ignaro are instead the ushers of the House of Holiness and Pride, whose functions are aesthetic: they represent the household at a liminal site. The usher to the House of Holiness, Reverence, is described in terms of simplicity that make him an unmistakably English Protestant saint:

There fayrely them receiues a gentle Squyre

Of myld demeanure, and rare courtesee,
Right cleanly clad in comely sad attire;
In word and deede that shewed great modestee,
And knew his good to all of each degree,
High *Reuerence*, He them with speeches meet
Does faire entreat; no courting nicetee,
But simple, trew, and eke vnfained sweet
As might become a Squyre so great persons to greet. (I. x. 7)

The stanza presents Reverence with plain style – here there is no complex syntax or vocabulary, and unity is emphasized through the assonance of key terms (demeanure, courtesee, cleanly, modestee, nicetee, sweet and greet), that also draws attention to the contrasting sound, and pause, on 'trew'. His resemblance to a 'Squyre' invokes images of bucolic hospitality that resonate with his 'comely sad attyre' and 'modestee'. Spenser borrows Virgilian associations of the rural landscape with virtue – a Roman pastoral[9] – and makes them markedly English: the scene and persona of Reverence is introduced by the image of the country Squire that sets the scene in an English landscape. The usher-Squire presents 'no courting nicetee', but rather 'simple, trew, and eke vnfained sweet', a pure sweetness that resonates with his 'cleanly clad'. Despite the lack of *apparent* difference between 'fained' and 'vnfained sweet', the mythology of simplicity holds up in the passage. The usher, like the House of Holiness's inhabitants, renders his moral and theological virtues in his appearance and simplicity is here synonymous with truthfulness and bucolic hospitality. The scene pre-empts Ben Jonson's celebration of the English countryhouse as the site of nature's, and the gentleman's, bounty in 'To Penshurst'.[10] As interiority becomes the privileged arena of sincerity and authenticity in Protestant England, so simplicity becomes the aesthetic guarantee of access to that interior. Fatoviç suggests a link between Protestant interiority and the significance of Catholicism's externality: 'To the extent that popery had come to represent a threatening exteriority, the internal became privileged, which goes some way towards explaining why interiority has become the proper locus of liberty' (p. 57). As Catholicism's danger was perceivable in its 'threatening exteriority', so Protestantism's plainness was an external guarantee of interiority.

As Linda Gregerson has noted, both Spenser and Milton present 'an epistemology and an epic peculiarly English and emphatically

Reformed' (p. 150). What Gregerson intimates here is the specific manifestation of Reformed theologies in Protestant England. Reformation theologies asserted the simplicity of Scripture to reveal a transcendent God, but they also asserted, heavily influenced by Calvin, a system of predestination in which the elect and reprobate were foreordained. Calvin's *Institutes*, published in English translation in 1561 posited a cosmic system, known as predestination, in which humanity was so tainted by sin that they were unable to turn to God of their own volition.[11] Not merely salvation but belief itself was an act of God. Only he could confer on the individual the grace to believe. Belief in God's utter omniscience meant that he had ordained, since before humanity's very creation, each individual's fate: undeserved salvation for the elect and deserved hell for the reprobate. It was a form of hyper-providentialism in which human agency was, theoretically (if not experientially), subsumed under divine will. A European movement, the Reformation took nationalist form especially in England, in which Calvinist theologies of election were quickly and adeptly applied to the people, not merely the individual. For radical Protestants, England had overtaken Israel as the chosen people of God, a view that untethered itself from specific Calvinist doctrine and became a widely espoused assertion. The Old Testament, favoured over the New by such Protestants, offered a narrative of national supremacy and drama. Adrian Hastings suggests:

> The Bible . . . presented in Israel itself a developed model of what it means to be a nation – a unity of people, language, religion, territory and government. Perhaps it was an almost terrifyingly monolithic ideal, productive ever after of all sorts of dangerous fantasies, but it was there, an all too obvious exemplar for Bible readers of what every other nation too might be, a mirror for national self-imagining.[12]

Even England's disasters would be read in the light of God's providential care for his chosen people. Richard Heyrick, for example, in a sermon given before the House of Commons in 1646 applies the text of 1 Kings 22. 19, in which God is chastising Israel, to England. Israel as chosen is also especially responsible, hence God's punishment is a sign of his peculiar care. Because exile was a result of God's wrath against Israel for its sins, Heyricke reads England's civil war as a sign of God's anger against his chosen people. Instead of Israel as the object of God's especial (albeit destructive) attention, Heyrick limns God asking 'shall I destroy *England?*'.[13] The peculiarly partisan national interpretation of Calvinism is apparent in John Stockwood's 1584 translation of the German John Brenz's commentary on the book of Esther, dedicated to Francis Walsingham. Brentz asserts universalism, following Luther's view of salvation which, in Hans Kohn's words, 'was a strictly individual concern which could be solved only by faith'.[14] For Brenz, the 'trve Israelites' are 'as many as beleeue in the seede of Abraham, which is Jesus Christ. This is the Church of Christ'.[15] Stockwood in striking contrast expresses a belief in England only as the new Israel. He claims that the English have 'the chifest places of credit, and countonance vnder Christian kinges and princes, not in the persecution, but the peace of the Gospell, not in the thraldome, but in the libertie of the church, not in the cloudes of ignorance, and the darke mist of superstition, but in the cleere light of the trueth, and bright shyning sunne of sincere religion'.[16] Catholics are vilified and the only true followers of Christ are the English.[17]

It was in the context of the emergence of such ideas, that are manifest so clearly later in the century and in the next, that Spenser writes. And it is as an *English* knight that Redcrossse possesses his new interpretive, redeemed ability. As well as Spenser's opening declaration of Elizabeth as 'Great Ladie of the greastest Isle' (1. Proem. 4), Redcrosse is given a heavenly vision that confirms his country's status as pre-eminent in the world. Although Redcrosse acknowledges London's type, Cleopolis, as secondary to the heavenly Jerusalem, his guide Contemplation asserts that London-Cleopolis is nonetheless 'for earthly frame,/ The fairest peece, that eie beholden can' (I. x. 59). Earth's inferiority to heavenly reality is asserted only to demonstrate London's relative value as superior to other earthly cities. It is in this scene that Redcrosse is revealed as St. George, cementing his status as representative of England: he is elect as Protestant but doubly so as a representative of Protestantism's leading nation, as many English saw themselves. Redcrosse's quest throughout the book is to rescue Una's parents, who it turns out are King and Queen of Eden (I. xii. 26), which means for Kermode that Redcrosse enacts the 'restoration of Eden' in England, linking Protestantism to the pastoral aesthetic.[18] Spenser's work thereby pre-empts the lineage of literary works that present England as the new Israel or Jerusalem.

Declaring Spenser the 'sage and serious Poet'[19], Milton carries forward the same nationalist and oppositional Protestant aesthetic as Spenser – of simplicity versus the ornamentation of Catholic ritual – and further weds it to the English landscape. Milton is no Calvinist, but his work demonstrates the widespread influence of Calvinist aesthetics, and especially in terms of the elect nation for which Milton is no less fervent than Spenser. 'Why else was this nation chos'n before any other', he states in his anti-censorship tract, *Areopagitica*, 'that out of her as out of *Sion* should be proclaim'd and sounded forth the first tidings and trumpet of Reformation to all *Europ*'. He states his conviction in revelation and in the English as its principal recipients: 'what does he then but reveal Himself to his servants, and as his manner is, first to his English-men?'.[20] If his political writings argue explicitly for freedom from censorship and liberty of conscience, then his long poem, *Paradise Lost*, presents these issues in narrative and aesthetic form. In a preface appended to its fourth issue, Milton presents the poem's simple literary form as a peculiarly English and moral trait, drawing his readers' attention to the relation between aesthetics, national identity and theology. Although never mentioned explicitly, it is simplicity that is indicated through his expulsion of the linguistic ornament of rhyme. Just as the throwing off of Catholic decoration in churches, and the eschewing of the more personal ornamentation of luxurious dress makes the Protestant free, so language is liberated by its eschewing of embellishment. As already noted, the image of throwing off entanglements was a familiar one in the Protestant lexicon. Milton identifies[21] his blank verse as 'English heroic verse without rhyme', claiming that 'rhyme being no necessary adjunct or true ornament of poem or good verse', but rather 'the invention of a barbarous age, to set off wretched matter and lame metre', that causes 'vexation, hindrance, and constraint'. His claim is grand: 'an example set, the first in English, of ancient liberty recovered to heroic poem from the troublesome and modern bondage of rhyming'.[22]

Milton partakes in and extends Spenser's anti-ritualism, rendering simplicity as Protestantism's haven. Milton describes Adam and Eve's 'evening worship' in book IV, which takes place in the natural world, naturalizing the act itself: 'under the open sky adored/ The God, that made both sky, air, earth and heaven' (IV. 721–2). Milton glosses the prayers they offer:

Thus said unanimous, and other rites
Observing none, but adoration pure
Which God likes best. (IV. 736–8)

The implication is that Adam and Eve can see and acknowledge God, can express 'adoration pure', because they are not constrained or obstructed by elaborate rites. United in their unanimous prayer, unencumbered, they can access a true perception of God's worth.

Like Spenser's poem, Milton's also demonstrates an adherence to Protestant ideals of transparency that are evident in the contrast of the plain speaking of God in book III and the deceptive rhetoric of Satan in books I and II and especially in his deception of Eve in book IX. Part of Milton's theodicy is to portray God as open and straightforward. While Satan works through 'deceit and lies' (V. 243), God instead discloses everything to Adam, through the angel Raphael, so that Adam is forewarned of Satan's attack. These respective linguistic styles are materialized in God's creation, the simple rurality of Eden, and the ornamented and artificial world of Satan's construction, the 'royal Seat', 'with pyramids and towers/ From diamond quarries hewn, and rocks of gold, The palace of great Lucifer' (V. 758–60). Pandemonium is 'like a Temple', 'with bossy Sculptures grav'n,/ The Roof was fretted Gold' (I. 716–17). Joseph Lyle notes the link between gold and hypocrisy commonly made in the early modern period (although based on a false etymology) that demonstrates the association of aesthetic, rhetoric and morality.[23] Lyle forcefully demonstrates that the construction of architecture and idolatry in *Paradise Lost* expresses Milton's objection to the way in which buildings can 'act as convenient loci to which idolatry, over time, will inevitably adhere', pointing to the archangel Michael's warning against Adam's desire to build 'grateful Altars' (XI. 323) that potentially limit God to geographical place. Lyle insists that Milton is wary of the fact that 'idolatry lurks in any artifact to which value can attach' (p. 139). Yet the inherent potential for idolatry in materiality is fulfilled in Milton's poem rather ironically in the English landscape itself. While Milton undercuts the relation between worship and constructed place (as Lyle magnificently outlines in his article), he instead renders an English countryside ripe for worship.

Even before he encounters Adam and Eve, Satan approaches the Garden of Eden. He finds there an exemplary form of the pastoral – he sees, for example, 'Flocks/ Grazing the tender herb' (IV. 252–3).

Milton's aesthetic, as was Spenser's, is heavily indebted to Virgilian images and convention, but his principal motive is to assert the claims of Protestantism. As Frank Kermode has argued, Milton 'cites Virgil and all other classics only to reject them, to explain that the new truth is different'.[24] This new truth pertains to Protestantism, but also the nation as England provides a source for Milton's aesthetics which means he infuses the landscape with a peculiarly English tinge. As John R. Knott notes, 'Adam and Eve practice a kind of gardening that would have been recognizable to Milton's contemporaries.'[25] Charlotte Otten outlines convincingly the relation between the English Garden and Milton's epic and their mutual reliance on the Genesis narrative (p. 250). Otten cites works contemporary to Milton that make the link explicit, such as the 1653 manual *The Garden of Eden, or An Accurate Description of all Flowers and Fruits now Growing in England* (p. 252). Milton's garden is, then, recognizably familiar to his English readers. Otten further states: 'It is Milton's willingness to incorporate in his "delicious Paradise" (IV. 132) some of the features of the actual gardens of his day and the practices of contemporary gardeners that makes him able to bridge the gap between the mythical and the real, between Art and Nature' (p. 253). Although other-worldly, a paradise lost, the landscape that Milton renders in his poem, then, is recognizably this-wordly. In consequence, not only humanity but the English countryside becomes touched with the divine. Dyrness notes that English taste for landscape demonstrates a Protestant veneration of nature.[26] Importantly, the landscape that Milton renders is that of the garden – the enclosed space where wildness is always within bounds and subject to cultivation. As England becomes 'this Eden', it is also markedly a tame, or to-be-tamed garden landscape. As such, the English as gardeners are controllers of the landscape in a way that corresponds to their assertion of self-control.

Milton's landscape is presented in a specifically Protestant form. Of especial note is the visit of the Archangel Raphael to Adam and Eve's rural bower which, as King has noted, is heavily infused with references to the eucharist. King suggests that Milton's invocation of the sacrament here demonstrates his emphasis upon interiority, but it also renders the English landscape simple (like the eucharist), and in its simplicity, theophanic. Here, the three enjoy an open-air picnic of earthly bounty:

> Raised of grassy turf
> Their table was, and mossy seats had round,
> And on her ample square from side to side
> All autumn piled . . . (V. 391–4)

Raphael eats the food Eve presents and is able to 'transubstantiate' (V. 438) it from 'corporeal to incorporeal' (V. 413), a clear parody of Catholic belief in real presence. The group's sitting and eating, while Eve 'ministered naked', presents in human nudity and open nature the pure, simple form of eucharistic celebration that had been outlined in the *Book of Common Prayer* (1660) and Westminster Assembly's *Directory for the Public Worship of God* (1644). King cites Milton's *Of Reformation* where he rails against the communion table having become 'a table of separation [. . .] fortified with balwark, and barricade, to keep off the profaine touch of the laicks', and suggests that Milton's allusions 'reinscribe accusations that High Church sacramentalism or the Roman Catholic Mass objectify spiritual truths that the Protestant Communion service renders internal and subjective' (p. 137). More pertinent in terms of the aesthetics rendered in Milton's scene is that the Protestant eucharist enacted a removal of barriers offering instead an accessible and open sacrament. As Otten notes, the 'mossy seat' was a favourite element of the English garden (p. 260) and as such, the rural scene becomes one in which the accessibility of God to the individual Protestant – direct divine communication rather than mediated access through priest – is infused in the English landscape.

Critics have noted a link between investment in the landscape and an untroubled hermeneutics of transparency. For example, Robert N. Watson states that 'the familiar efforts to recover simple experience out in the fields or in the wilderness, to re-immerse oneself in the natural order, were partly fuelled by a craving for unmediated knowledge in any form'.[27] Milton's return to the creation narrative was a grasping after a Scriptural and temporal foundation, as Watson notes regarding landscape writing: 'As the persistent references to the Garden of Eden suggest, the movement back to nature was partly a code for a drive back toward some posited certainty' (p. 3). And as England was increasingly invoked as 'This other Eden', it was the English landscape, more specifically, that rendered the divine voice. While the material human body is 'fleshly', tainted by Adam and Eve's sin, the natural world and the mind continue as the locus of divine communication. The mind that reads the natural world is divorced from the body that senses, acts and feels, and as such rationality becomes reified as the site of privileged truth and certainty, while the natural world remains the site of divine revelation.

As apparent in the scene with Adam, Eve and Raphael, nudity is a clear sign of simplicity's signifying of authenticity, purity and transparency. Eve who 'ministered naked' is also described 'in naked beauty more adorned,/ More lovely than Pandora, whom the gods/ Endowed with all their gifts' (IV. 713–15). The Edenic state of nature and nudity represents a meeting of innocence, simplicity and transparency, a nexus of beliefs that coalesced in the early modern period under the figure of the 'noble savage'. Aphra Behn, a Catholic and royalist, in her lengthy description of the 'Indians' in her *Oroonoko* of 1688, likens their wearing of bead 'Aprons' 'as Adam and Eve did the Fig-leaves' and who she explicitly states 'represented to me an absolute Idea of the first State of Innocence, before Man knew how to sin'.[28] She presents them as transparent signifiers of this innocence, layering up references to her own penetrating vision:

> being continually us'd to see one another so unadorn'd, so like our first Parents before the Fall, it seems as if they had no Wishes; there being nothing to heighten Curiosity, but all you can see, you see at once, and every Moment see[.] (pp. 7–8)

With her 'all', 'at once' and 'every Moment', Behn underlines the totality, the immediacy and the pervasiveness of her own perception, but it also tells of the superlative level of disclosure – everything is revealed, at once and always. Nature demonstrates the self-evident, transparent and virtuous qualities of simplicity:

> And 'tis most evident and plain, that simple Nature is the most harmless, inoffensive and vertuous Mistress. 'Tis she alone, if she were permitted, that better instructs the World, than all the Inventions of Man: Religion wou'd here but destroy that Tranquillity, they possess by Ignorance; and Laws wou'd but teach 'em to know Offence, of which now they have no Notion. (pp. 8–9)

Within a text that explores the complexity of factual truth, there is nonetheless an assertion of the transparency of simplicity, and a return to Eden as a site of exemplary knowledge. Only Nature can imbue the Indians with a simplicity of Edenic innocence, a nature beyond the 'invention' of religion and law, cultural structures only needed in the face of postlapsarian Original Sin, as the Catholic Behn would define it. Behn's articulation of what I have called a 'Protestant aesthetic' indicates the degree to which simplicity becomes a cultural norm and that English Catholicism expresses a distaste for 'religion' (synonymous at this time with ritual) and a privileging of the transparent and simple. What has its home in Protestant theology soon becomes a more widely applicable principle, as will be explored in the next chapter.

CHAPTER TWO

SECULARIZING THE PROTESTANT AESTHETIC

In the sixteenth and seventeenth centuries simplicity was informed quite consciously by radical Protestant theologies of the transparency of Scripture, the Calvinist 'spectacles' that God bestowed on the elect that made them the discerning, rational and self-controlled elite. At the start of the eighteenth century it was still an aesthetic directly informed by anti-Catholic sentiment, but as the eighteenth century drew to a close, simple aesthetics became increasingly untethered from the specific theological context from which they gained their significance. As the signifieds of simplicity became naturalized, so it began to function not as an expression of Protestant values, but instead as a marker against which moral values were measured. Simplicity came to embody virtue.

The oppositional force of anti-Catholicism was still, for some time, influential. Joseph Addison, co-founder of *The Spectator* Magazine (1711–12), sets the simple and natural explicitly against Catholic ostentation. In writing on the respective 'Manners' of city and country, he asserts that by manners, 'I do not mean morals, but behaviour and good breeding', privileging exteriority over inward principles.[1] He considers the elaboration of polite forms and ceremonies to have become 'like the *Romish* religion', 'so encumbered with show and ceremony, that it stood in need of a reformation to retrench its superfluities, and restore it to its natural good sense and beauty' (p. 196). 'Romish' elaborate manners, like their religious counterpart, are in need of reforming to purge them of their debilitating pomposity and to restore them to a state of nature, simplicity and good sense. It was an aesthetic set of associations widely accepted in the period and a key signifier for English self-identification. Samuel Johnson, for example, writes of Addison's as a model of 'English style', 'elegant but not ostentatious', utilizing the implicitly anti-Catholic notion of rejected ornamentation both to praise and indicate Englishness.[2] In the nineteenth century, Calvinist-influenced writers such as Thomas Carlyle prioritized simplicity. He praises the English for their 'talent of silence', expressed in the simple style of poetics, echoing Milton's rejection of linguistic excess: 'Great honour to him whose Epic is a melodious hexameter Iliad; not a jingling Sham-Iliad, nothing true in it but the hexameters and forms merely'.[3]

Jeremy Black claims that in the eighteenth century anti-Catholicism was 'arguably the prime ideological commitment of most of the population'.[4] The rejection of ostentation and ritual is given continuing impetus from the sense of the Englishman's distance from his Catholic neighbours and simplicity continues as an outworking of still-virulent anti-Catholic sentiment. Ihalainen's study of Protestant England notes that 'anti-Catholicism declined dramatically in mid-eighteenth-century definitions of the English nation' (2005, p. 21), although Clement Fatović traces 'the rhetoric of anti-popery' in Locke and other eighteenth-century writers which, he argues, 'still proved quite useful in explaining the exceptionalism of English freedom' into the second half of the century ('Anti-Catholic Roots', p. 50). As far as articulating Englishness was concerned, it seems that anti-Catholicism remained influential for some time, yet to identify it as an explicit doctrine in late eighteenth- and nineteenth-century discourse in England becomes increasingly difficult. While anti-Catholicism wavered doctrinally, the oppositional impulse was apparent and proved durable in the aesthetic realm.

This chapter considers the aesthetic of simplicity in the eighteenth and nineteenth centuries, outlining its function as a primarily oppositional aesthetic that denigrates both external and internal enemies. Scholarship on simplicity in the eighteenth century is most often considered in terms of its Classical sources. I demonstrate how attention to its classical background has left simplicity's heritage in Reformed ideas neglected, arguing instead that religious motivations are overlooked because their very ubiquity in the eighteenth century means they are rarely explicitly articulated. A turn to considering its religious influences is important because otherwise simplicity's inherently oppositional force can be left invisible. Although emerging from a Reformed Protestant context, simplicity takes on a life of its own, becoming so authoritative that it even works to authorize (rather than being cognate with) theological positions.

The secularization thesis of a trajectory from theology to morality is tempered by attention to aesthetics, which are revealed as central to understanding the persistence of Protestant oppositionality within mythologies of Englishness. The chapter ends with readings of the embeddedness of aesthetics of English simplicity in the landscape and representative characters in Wordsworth's *The Excursion*, George Eliot's *Adam Bede* and *Middlemarch* and Thomas Hardy's *Far from the Madding Crowd*.

Simplicity continued to function as a marker of election: taste for the simple set the tasteful apart as superior, not only in national terms – as the English against (usually Catholic) foreigners – but it also worked effectively to mark internal opposition, setting apart the 'true' English from inferior classes. As Addison continues his analysis of breeding, setting apart the ostentatious from the natural, he simultaneously demarcates the tasteful from flawed imitators. He outlines the problems of the new and deceptively straightforward fashion of 'openness': 'good breeding shows itself most, where to an ordinary eye it appears the least', he claims. The simple aesthetics of good breeding belie the need for the extraordinary reader to discern its presence. The supposedly natural countryside folk are recognizable by their excess of ceremonial, the result of their misreading of what makes good breeding. They ape their city neighbours in an outdated mode because they are not able to discern the nuances of refined manners that 'to the ordinary eye' are indecipherable.

Simplicity continues to communicate the full range of Protestant qualities outlined in the previous chapter: superiority, transparency, rationality and self-possession. In his economy of good breeding, Addison presents the self-possessed man as the ideal. The man who is cheerful possesses a 'moral habit of mind' that enables him to be 'a perfect master of all the powers and faculties of his soul. His imagination is always clear, and his judgment undisturbed. His temper is even and unruffled'.[5] Here, as in Spenser's and Milton's nexus of the aesthetic of simplicity, clarity (of imagination) is allied with temperance and self-control: discernment leads intuitively to control of one's environment and oneself.

Addison's hugely influential journal pieces demonstrate a faith in nature and in representation as a transparent medium. Regarding a song 'of the common people', he asserts that 'This song is a plain simple copy of nature, destitute of the helps and ornaments of art', again utilizing the antagonistic duality of simplicity versus ornament.[6]

Even though simplicity is multivalent, signifying a host of different and often contrasting qualities (from stupidity to tastefulness), the myth of simplicity's transparency is nonetheless tenacious. Although Addison speaks of the song's 'despicable simplicity' (p. 24) at first, he goes on to identify the reader who gleans beauty in simplicity as exemplary: 'only those who are endowed with a true greatness of soul and genius, can divest themselves of the little images of ridicule, and admire nature in her simplicity and nakedness' (pp. 25–6). Simplicity, at first vulgar when applied to crude writing, becomes the marker of naked and, the implication is, truthful and virtuous nature. Addison's writing is full, unsurprisingly, of recommendations towards nature: to women to 'follow your natural modesty', for example.[7] Marjorie Garson in her study, *Moral Taste*, reflects on the paradoxical function of taste for the natural (and by extension the simple) as a marker of the elite: taste is 'a kind of unmediated emanation of their refinement of spirit', she observes (p. 5). She finds the contradiction puzzling: 'Despite the interest Burke takes in universal psychological and emotional responses, he does not finally endorse the "natural taste" of any but the most highly developed individuals' (p. 9). Garson identifies the discretion at play in aesthetics, remarking: 'Taste is evidently like grace in the Calvinist sense: those who can respond to beauty are the elect; those who cannot, the reprobate' (p. 13). Although she uses the language of Reformation theology, it is for Garson merely a metaphor as she 'brackets the theological dimension of the problem' (p. 13), a garment that merely clothes the core of taste for simplicity. As such the source of simplicity's complex logic in Reformed theology is tantalizingly gestured towards but ultimately neglected. As this chapter seeks to demonstrate, it is not merely election but opposition to elaborate aesthetics and their counterparts of irrationality and lack of control that simplicity retains from its Reformed heritage. To ignore its theological grounding is to neglect the full spectrum of simplicity's significance as a sign of Englishness.

Simplicity has become a subject of critical interest for scholars of the eighteenth century. As Raymond D. Havens outlines, simplicity shifts significance across the period:

the simplicity of the neoclassicists had been largely intellectual, critical, restrictive, and Latinic, concerned with literature, with propriety and regularity, tending to be elegant and sophisticated,

whereas the simplicity of later eighteenth century [sic] was enthusiastic and emotional; it was inspired by the Greeks and looked
back [. . .] to life, to the ideal beauty and vitality of joyous
Athenian youth. (Havens, p. 25)

Simplicity's morphing from a regulated and elegant neoclassicism to
an emotional manifestation indicates its complexity, but its changing
nuances of emphasis are nonetheless subject to the larger paradigm
of the theological emphasis of transparency and its related qualities,
rationalism and freedom. A later example will serve to illustrate
the tenacity of simplicity's entanglement with transparency, even in
writing that engages with its hermeneutic and logical complexities.
Carlyle, a writer hugely influenced by Scottish Calvinism, plays with
the slipperiness of simplicity and its significations only, at the final
analysis, to stabilize it. In his comparison of the Man of Practice
and the Man of Theory, he appears at first to set simplicity and
transparency at odds:

How one loves to see the burly figure of him, this thick-skinned,
seemingly opaque, perhaps sulky, almost stupid Man of Practice,
pitted against some light adroit Man of Theory, all equipt with
clear logic, and able anywhere to give you Why for Wherefore! The
adroit Man of Theory, so light of movement, clear of utterance,
with his bow full-bent and quiver full of arrow-arguments, – surely
he will strike down the game, transfix everywhere the heart of the
matter; triumph everywhere, as he proves that he shall and must
do? (*Past and Present*, p. 199)

In Carlyle's delineation of the Man of Practice, the stereotype of the
simple life, references to opacity layer up: cloudy, thick, in silence.
Instead the 'light' and 'clear' Man of Theory should win the day. But
Carlyle's intention is suggested in his use of 'seemingly', which we
saw in Spenser is a term that divides visual from ontological reality.
He explains the Man of Practice's opacity as one that does not veil
understanding, but the cloudy, thick, opaque silence instead 'transcends all logic-utterance' and in doing so exists on the same plain as
Carlyle's mysterious and sublime 'Unuttered':

To your astonishment, it turns out oftenest No. The cloudy-
browed, thick-soled, opaque Practicality, with no logic utterance,

in silence mainly, with here and there a low grunt or growl, has in him what transcends all logic-utterance: a Congruity with the Unuttered. The Speakable, which lies atop, as a superficial film, or outer skin, is his or is not his: but the Doable, which reaches down to the World's centre, you find him there! (p. 199)

The clarity and light of the Man of Logic is merely 'a superficial film', he is a fragile man of surfaces. Instead, the Man of Practice 'reaches down to the World's centre'. The relation between simplicity and transparency is maintained, despite Carlyle's use of visual metaphors of hiddenness. Transparency is instead rendered in material terms as profundity: the Man of Theory may appear light and clear, but he is so shallow that he is in fact opaque. Conversely, the Man of Practice, appearing opaque, contains no surface, is utterly transcendent 'to the world's centre'. Carlyle here sums up the paradoxical movement of simplicity: at once transcendent and viscerally earthy, it is both divine and 'truly real'.

Where classical sources of simplicity are widely identified in scholarship on the eighteenth century, religious sources often remain marginal in terms of critical engagement. Although the classics were primary and vital sources of simplicity, its force as a virtue came from Protestantism. Reformed characteristics are apparent in Thomas Blackwell's attitude to Homeric simplicity and simple manners, which:

have a peculiar Effect upon the Language, not only as they are natural, but as they are ingenuous and *good*. While a Nation continues simple and sincere, whatever they say has *Weight* from *Truth*: Their Sentiments are strong and honest; which always produce fit Words to express them: Their Passions are sound and genuine, not adulterated or disguised, and break out in their own artless Phrase and unaffected Stile. They are not accustomed to *Prattle*, and little pretty *Forms* that enervate a polished Speech.[8]

Fred Parker in his essay 'Classic Simplicity' – that deftly analyses issues of the translation of simplicity – links Blackwell's attitudes to Enlightenment 'unease with modernity' (p. 229) and reads it against the '"doubleness" and artifice of his own time and culture' (p. 230). But in this quotation we see the relation between the durability of English national success, transparency, honesty and discernment (finding fit words), set against what would have been recognized as a

Popish elaborate yet empty style (prattle) and deceit (disguise). Parker references the biblical in relation to the dual sources of Scripture and the *Iliad* for Pope yet only considers Homeric simplicity. Parker states that, for Blackwell, 'the classic text is a magic portal into a world of value otherwise inaccessible and lost' (p. 230). Blackwell's sense of the transparency of poetry parallels Protestant assumptions about the perspicuity of Scripture for the redeemed reader. As will be discussed later in the chapter, an articulation of a Protestant corpus of qualities, when mapped onto the English landscape and on notions of Englishness, is more durable outside the literary than Parker acknowledges.

Classical myopia is more pronounced in Raymond Havens' excellent (and still influential) 1953 survey of simplicity in the eighteenth and nineteenth centuries, 'Simplicity, a Changing Concept'.[9] He explicitly traces only classical influences on articulations of simplicity in politicians, philosophers and poets: 'it was inseparably linked with two authorities held in the highest reverence: nature and the Ancients' (p. 5). Many of Havens' numerous citations have an implicit religious dimension, and he does engage with religious manifestations of simplicity, as in footnote 35 which comments on 'Simplicity in preaching, which had been a burning issue in the seventeenth century'. Although religion is not critically engaged with, Protestantism is the unacknowledged ever-present influence in the article, manifesting itself tellingly when Havens wants to defend Wordsworth's simplicity against accusations of childishness. In true Protestant style, he turns to the Bible as ultimate authority. He comments, turning to Mark 10.15: ' "Whosoever shall not receive the kingdom of God as a little child," declared the Master, "he shall not enter therein" ' (p. 30). Havens' nonchalance in deferring to 'the Master' within academic discourse jars now in a way that seemingly did not occur to Havens, and one presumes his readers, in the 1950s. That classical sources, but not the Bible, are subject to critical reflection demonstrates how far the religious elements of simplicity have been unduly neglected. Simplicity is positioned in a classical literary heritage, which, because of its apparent longevity and ideological neutrality, naturalizes simplicity's moral associations and ignores the moment of its construction in Protestant doctrine. As an historically and Marxist oriented discipline over the past thirty years, English Studies may have privileged Classical sources over the ideologically fraught Bible, but in doing so it has often overlooked Protestantism's ongoing oppositional aesthetic force.

Admittedly, simplicity's specific post-Reformation significance is difficult to discern as it becomes an aesthetic increasingly separated from its theological grounding. Even in theological contexts, simplicity takes on a mythological life of its own – functioning, in Barthes' terms, as a second-order sign (see Introduction, p. 19). Simplicity becomes not the aesthetic or marker of Reformation transparency, but theology is measured by its adherence to an aesthetics of simplicity. The Christian Socialist F. D. Maurice in 1855 appeals to the 'witness' of 'simplicity' in his 'The Communion Service' to verify his theological position:

> But are we investing the bread and the wine with some magical properties? Are we supposing that they admit us into a Presence, which but for them would be far from us? Do they not rather bear witness, by their simplicity, by their universality, that it is *always* near to us, near to every one.

The apparently magical properties of the sacrament are transferred to simplicity as a sign of the unmediated presence of God, a guarantor of transparency and presence. Throughout his pamphlet, Maurice elaborates on the elements of the eucharistic service, asserting quite explicitly their mutual simplicity and transparency: 'Surely what we need is, that they should be made a perfectly transparent medium, through which His glory may be manifested'. Maurice goes on to articulate the movement of the eucharist from an everyday context to one 'purely sacramental', in which it becomes a transparent communicator of divine meaning:

> For this end the elements require a solemn consecration from the priest [. . .] – that they may be diverted from their ordinary uses, – that they may become purely sacramental. No doubt the world is full of sacraments. Morning and evening, the kind looks and parting words of friends, the laugh of childhood, daily bread, sickness and death, all have a holy sacramental meaning [. . .] But then they have another meaning, which keeps this out of sight. If we would have them translated to us, we need some pure untroubled element, which has no significancy, except as the organ through

which the voice of God speaks to man, and through which he may answer, 'Thy servant heareth.'

Such we believe are this bread and wine, when redeemed to His service. Let us not deprive them of their ethereal whiteness and clearness, by the colours of our fancy, or the clouds of our intellect.[10]

Maurice wants to set aside bread and wine from their everyday associations and instead present them as a 'pure untroubled element', separate from the world and made sacred, as identified in their 'ethereal whiteness and clearness'. Modified by his earlier descriptor of 'simplicity', the elements become unfettered, clear communicators of the divine.

Maurice's recourse to simplicity as an arbitrator reflects an ongoing Protestant rejection of ostentation, illustrated in the protest by a group of Dorset laymen regarding their 'deep anxiety' about the increased 'Ornaments and Ritualistic practices almost identical with those of the Church of Rome', in response to the practices of the Bishop of Salisbury, W. K. Hamilton, who was notably 'sympathetic to ritual innovation'.[11] Their letter in February 1867 to the Earl of Shaftesbury deems the rituals 'repugnant to, the Scriptural Simplicity of Protestant worship'. The 'Scriptural Simplicity' is then qualified as the 'pure doctrines of Gospel truth', simplicity becoming synonymous with purity, itself typified in a Protestant gospel. They end by claiming that these rituals 'undermine the Protestant foundations of the Established Church, and endanger, within these realms, the very existence of the Reformation itself'.[12] The aesthetic force of Reformation theologies, then, was apparent in certain corners of England. Alec R. Vidler illustrates their wider influence as he reflects on ritualism's national impulse in his *The Church in an Age of Revolution* that: 'the ordinary Englishman likes, or thinks he likes, simplicity in religion, and dislikes elaboration and sophistication'.[13] Louis E. Daniels traces an ongoing link between the theology of eucharistic practice and dress (seen in chapter 1 in extreme form in Milton's Eve's 'ministered naked', see p. 45): 'Those who held the continental view of the Eucharistic Presence refused utterly to assume a garment which implied that Presence. Many insisted on ministering in their street clothes, or peasant's jacket, and we have record of one priest who felt that he must wear his hat during the service.'[14]

Although now following its own trajectory, Protestant aesthetics of simplicity without doubt received a boost from the vibrant Protestant movements, such as Methodism, that still advocated the virtues of simplicity, lack of ritual and that presumed rationalism and freedom as concomitants of their faith. But as seen in Maurice and Ritualism, even in theological debate simplicity is a discrete value, testing and not expressing, theological positions. Protestantism was still hugely influential into the nineteenth and even the twentieth century, with evangelicals such as Gladstone and Balfour holding key political positions. Yet over the next few centuries, simplicity as a marker of the elect increasingly becomes an aesthetic value that is dominant over religious or doctrinal mores.

Again, the focus on the aesthetic realm as the carrier of Protestant oppositional logic is crucial to understand its persistence to the present day. Where arguments and even Protestant-inspired moralities eventually wane and are subject to argument, the aesthetic of simplicity has continued above the fray of secularizing logics. Scholarship on the influence of Protestantism on literary constructions of England frequently refers to the *moral* heritage of England's Protestant past. In his book, *Nation and Novel*, Patrick Parrinder intricately traces the 'puritan temper' in the novels of Emily Brontë, George Eliot and Thomas Hardy, delineating a set of characteristics that he takes from J. R. Green's *Short History of England*, namely, 'independence, moral fervour, social or at least spiritual egalitarianism, domestic tenderness, and sobriety of speech and costume'.[15] Parrinder identifies, for example, the 'life of self-denial and Puritanical rectitude' of Felix Holt (p. 275) and sets Dorothea Brooke as the Puritan against Will Ladislaw, Casaubon's 'somewhat Cavalier relative', a comparison historicized in the opposing personalities of the English civil war (p. 277). The novels present a 'rural paganism' and 'a contrast of Cavalier and Puritan types' (p. 280), a Puritanism of character traits that does not 'necessarily mean a religious affiliation' (p. 280). Using as his key examples Jude and Angel Clare, Parrinder outlines a Puritanism of moral compunction that follows the familiar trajectory of the nineteenth-century secularization of theology into morality. Parrinder talks of Angel Clare's 'scruples of the Puritan conscience' that he has in his 'Pauline morality', an 'admiration of "spotlessness" and hatred of "impurity"' (*Tess*, p. 256), and as such gestures towards the aesthetics of post-Puritan morality (as he does with the already-cited 'sobriety of speech and costume'). But Parrinder is dealing overwhelmingly with the moral overhang of a religious upbringing – with a hatred of moral impurity, Tess's lack of chastity – rather than considering the wider cultural aesthetic that breeds dispositions to and against the visually spotless and pure, an aesthetic that although morally implicated registers on a purely aesthetic level.

It is also important to note that Protestantism's theological influence was relatively stronger in terms of ideas of national identity than in the wider cultural sphere. This may explain why English mythologies of simplicity have been especially persistent. The marriage of English nationhood and Calvinist ideas of election continued, albeit in an increasingly secularist framework. Colin Haydon argues in his chapter in *Protestantism and National Identity* that the continuing popularity of Foxe's Protestant propaganda, *Acts and Monuments,* in the eighteenth century worked to sustain the 'belief that the English were an elect people'.[16] Whereas Calvinism as an active theological force was in the minority in England, as Anthony Smith points out in *Theories of Nationalism*, even as late as 1836, the *Oxford English Dictionary* defined nationalism in theological terms, with nations the object of divine election.[17] This notion of election was one communicated most tenaciously in the form of innocent yet oppositional simplicity.

The reception of Milton in the eighteenth and nineteenth centuries was dominated by just such Reformed constructions of taste. As King notes, *Paradise Lost* was accepted as a 'sublime masterpiece standing above the fray of history', its divine aesthetic presenting ahistorical verities for English self-identification.[18] Addison's definitions of literary taste, so shaped by Reformed and anti-Catholic assumptions as we have seen, became the dominant lens through which Milton's representation of rural simplicity was received, perhaps most importantly in Wordsworth's poetry.

Returning to the complementary relationship between aesthetics and dispositions (see p. 21–6), it is important to note that Milton's, or Wordsworth's, influence on notions of simplicity was not merely an intellectual one. Certain aesthetic assertions also constructed specific dispositions, in particular towards the English landscape. The lines of influence from Spenser to Milton, to Wordsworth, to Hardy, Eliot and Orwell, are strongly established, but they did not occur merely within the pages of books. Influence was not only from author to author but was kept alive by an active readership that shaped the canon that in turn embraced these writers, and brought their writings into the wider culture and material world. These writers were not torch-bearers for a specific idea, but reflected and refracted, in specific and often seemingly contradictory ways, wider cultural assumptions surrounding visual (and conceptual) simplicity. We know that as individuals read these authors' works, they often enacted the dispositions the works encouraged. Stephen Gill opens his book on *Wordsworth and the Victorians* on the various pilgrimages that Victorian individuals made to the sites of Wordsworthian poetry, ritually enacting response to place.[19] For example he notes that Tennyson like many others visited Bolton Abbey, the scene of *The White Doe of Rylstone*, 'his "imagination inflamed" by Wordsworth's poem' (p. 2). In his study, Gill brings to our attention not simply readers but 'their acts' (p. 3). Literature is never purely rational and for the writers considered in this study, literature works upon the reader. It is a thoroughly Protestant assumption: Thomas Cranmer writes in the *Book of Homilies* that 'he that is most inspired with the holy ghost most in his harte and life, altered and transformed into that thing, which he readeth'.[20] Spenser believed he was fashioning a gentleman, and Stanley Fish has outlined how Milton constructs the reader as a 'participant in the action', culpable in her own attraction to Satanic wiles.[21] In this chapter we engage with Wordsworth, who outlines a supra-rational transferral of feeling in poetry, and Eliot and Hardy who engage with the visceral logic of human conviction and action (see discussion in Introduction, pp. 25–6).

Gill's book on Wordsworth's influence is rare in advocating a form of sympathetic, even salvatory reading, in which emotional, not cognitive or critical, resonance is given precedence. Before the twentieth century, readers were explicit about expecting moral instruction on how to live. Wordsworth's poems especially were often conceptualized by their readers in Scriptural terms. In other words, they were frequently valued as proximate to the Bible in terms of their spiritual nourishment: 'the world has no poetry outside the Bible that can stand a comparison with his in this respect' states Henry Hudson.[22] John Wilson, poet and contributor to *Blackwood's Edinburgh Magazine* claimed Wordsworth's was 'the book which I value next to my Bible'.[23] Like the Bible, Wordsworth's poetry was perceived as having a potentially transforming and sanctifying effect. Gill encourages this priority of emotion over criticism in the final lines of his introduction: 'Within university departments of English such a mode of reading is regarded as old-fashioned at best, suspect and misguided at worst, but it is still more common, and more valued in the wider world than professors suppose' (p. 4).

Wordsworth expresses what seems to have been an intuitive link in Protestant England in reiterating the ties between simplicity, transcendence, rationality and control, so evident in Addison, but applies them almost exclusively to the ordinary man and his rural landscape. Havens comments that Wordsworth, 'as regards simplicity, was the most influential and important nineteenth-century English writer' (p. 27). The 1802 Preface to *Lyrical Ballads* provides a frame of simplicity through which to read his poetic work, in which simple 'nature' is contrasted to 'manners' (l. 203–4) and through which Wordsworth intertwines simplicity and authenticity, invoking implicitly a Protestant construction of simplicity:

> Low and rustic life was generally chosen, because in that condition the essential passions of the heart find a better soil in which they can attain their maturity, are less under restraint, and speak a plainer and more emphatic language; because in that condition of life our elementary feelings co-exist in a state of greater simplicity, and consequently, may be more accurately contemplated and more forcibly communicated; because the manners of rural life germinate from those elementary feelings and, from the necessary character of rural occupations, are more easily comprehended, and are more durable; and lastly, because in that condition the passions of men are incorporated with the beautiful and permanent forms of nature. [24]

Dwelling in the natural world nurtures passions in such as way as to enable their purer articulation. Rural practice and authentic, pure feelings are organically related to the landscape, painting a picture of rurality in which practice, feelings and landscape co-exist. The image is of life stripped back to its 'elementary' – and thereby purer, plain and more comprehensible – foundation, a trope of naked authenticity that Wordsworth uses in a letter in 1802 to John Wilson: 'by stripping our own hearts naked, and by looking out of ourselves to[wards men] who led simplest lives, and those most according to nature; men who have never known false refinements'.[25]

Wordsworth is heavily indebted to Milton, 'the Bard, Holiest of Men' and in such a way as to perpetuate Reformed attitudes to Englishness.[26] In book IX of *The Excursion*, the most popular of his works for the Victorians, Wordsworth appears to invoke both Satan's first view of Adam and Eve and the scene of the meal that they host for the Archangel Raphael, discussed in chapter 1, with all of its connotations of the simultaneous transparency and virtue of nature. The passage in *The Excursion* (ll. 420–559) comes immediately after the musings of the Wanderer on the state of 'Merry England' (l. 175), an England to be ameliorated by education and progressive industrialization, but also by its landscape, 'the infinite magnificence of heaven,/ Within the reach of every human eye' (IX. 210–11). English landscape is divine and England is elect, the Wanderer giving a call to action with the cry: 'Your Country must complete/ Her glorious destiny' (ll. 410–11). Wordsworth subtly invokes *Paradise Lost* in recourse to the 'mandate from above' (l. 369) for fruitfulness, bringing to mind its Edenic situation. Here, in the 'upright form' (l. 211) of man, Wordsworth refers to the scene of Satan's first view of God's principal creation, Adam and Eve, but applies it to the stunning spectacle of a 'snow-white Ram', a figure infused with biblical resonances of purity and of Abraham's sacrifice of Isaac, a type of Christ in Protestant hermeneutics. The landscape echoes Miltonic language. The scene of Adam and Eve, 'Raised of grassy turf/ Their table was and mossy seats had round' (V. 391–2) is echoed in the 'grassy bank' (IX. 443) and 'green turf' (IX. 444). Attention to the Ram's 'imperial front' (IX. 446), 'Shaggy and bold, and wreathed horns superb' (447) echoes the attention to Adam's 'fair large front' (IV. 3000), expressing 'Absolute rule' and his 'hyacinthine locks' (IV. 301, which 'manly hung/ Clustering' (IV. 302–3). We see in the Ram's reflection in the rivulet a 'two-fold Image', suggesting the duality of the 'gentlest pair' (IV. 366) of representative humanity in whom 'The image of their glorious maker shone' (IV. 292). Wordsworth imparts to the snow-white Ram, not humanity, the Christ-image of incarnation and carrier of the divine image. The reflected Ram takes the place of pre-eminence as the creature who expresses God's immanence and 'seemed centre of his own fair world' (l. 451). Bestial nature is the vessel of divine revelation, humanity instead the 'broken company' (IX. 435). Not only nature, but speech carries something of an Edenic transparency in this scene. The Pastor's wife reflects on the ability of the Wanderer to articulate sublime realities as she whispers that she loves to hear 'that eloquent Old Man' because 'While he is speaking I have the power to see/ Even as he sees'; prophetic vision is imparted to poetic utterance. Wordsworth constructs an Edenic paradise as the group stop to picnic. The Wanderer asserts prelapsarian innocence – 'we cannot err/ In this delicious Region' (IX. 504–5) – and the group's picnicking is accompanied by a 'simple song' (IX. 534) and 'stiller sounds' (IX. 533). Miltonic 'nature boon/ Poured forth profuse' (*Paradise Lost*, IV. 242–3) as the Wanderer exclaims 'Rapaciously we gathered flowery spoils/ From land and water' (*Excursion* IX. 538–9). That it is ultimately a transient paradise is suggested in the Pastor's wife's lament over the moment's fragility and the Solitary's sorrow over the loss of the innocent pleasure, 'an emblem here/ Of one day's pleasure, and all mortal joys!' (IX. 554–5). The strongly Miltonic term 'mortal' simultaneously insinuates fallenness in the 'forbidden tree' of 'mortal taste' (I. 2) and redemption in his description of God's call for one to become 'mortal to redeem/ Man's mortal crime' (III. 214–15).

The group move on to a 'mossy stone' where they 'sate reclined' invoking more strongly the scene of Adam, Eve and Raphael's meal, 'Raised of grassy turf/ Their table was and mossy seats had round' (V. 391–2). The group's scene is also a communal, heavenly one of sharing the joys of a 'rapturous moment', suggesting spiritual epiphany, a passage filled with Miltonic references (see notes in Bushell, Butler and Jaye). But, again, the focus is the natural world, not the human. The skies, like Adam, Eve and the Archangel, are in 'prodigal communion', the reflection of the 'unapparent fount of glory' asserting the trace of the divine realm, echoing the sublimity and perfection of the ram's watery image, using a rare term, 'unapparent', used by Milton at the point of creation, 'the rising birth/ Of nature from the unapparent deep' (VII. 103). English landscape becomes infused with Miltonic strains, but carries forward a set of assumptions about rurality, simplicity and divine revelation that impart on the dweller of that landscape an organic relation to 'speak a plainer and emphatic language' that we will see echoed in twentieth-century literature of rural England. For Wordsworth, the transparency assumed in nature is related, through Milton, to a Protestant hermeneutic that is strongly biblical and linked explicitly to reclamation of prelapsarian communion with God. Englishness is almost synonymous with a divinely permeated landscape. Coleridge states that: 'We see our God everywhere – the Universe in the most literal Sense is his written language', an assertion applicable to a wide range of religious positions (a spectrum that Coleridge himself moved along), and as such an assumption that becomes curiously widespread in later secular representations of England.[27]

In recent scholarship, the identification of England with the countryside is often explained in historical terms as a response to the expansion of Empire and its perceived threats to local identity. In his *An Imaginary England: Landscape and Literature 1840–1920*, for example, Roger Ebbatson argues that:

> The expansive project of empire is accompanied, dialectically, by a narrowing and intensification of an Englishness predicated in terms of landscape, a trope of naming that unifies and smoothes out regional and topographical difference. [28]

The myth of simplicity is indeed fuelled by a sense of the overwhelming complexities of Empire, but it gains its imaginative strength from the mythologies of Milton's Edenic landscape that contain the Reformation's assertion of the transparency of the world for the redeemed reader. The Edenic focus is important as England is persistently envisioned explicitly or implicitly in terms of a paradisiacal *garden*. Addison expresses the significance of the garden within notions of Englishness:

> A garden was the habitation of our first parents before the fall. It is naturally apt to fill the mind with calmness and tranquillity, and to lay all its turbulent passions at rest. It gives us great insight into the contrivance and wisdom of providence[.][29]

The garden, like Addison's simplicity, communicates clarity in terms of being unfettered from strife and passion, as well as hermeneutically translucent, giving one privileged access to the divine will. Bucolic England is frequently characterized by a temperance that is both telling of the paradisiacal nature of Eden and of the moderateness of true Englishness. At a time in which climate was considered constitutive of human nature (it was widely believed that moving climates would result in changes of skin colour and physiognomy), demonstration of England's temperate climate was proof enough of Englishmen's self-possession. In the eighteenth century, John Reinhold Forster, who travelled with Captain James Cook on

Resolution wrote in 1778 that he saw 'the powerful influence of climate, food, and peculiar customs upon the colour, size, habit, and
form of body; and certain defects, excesses, or modifications of the
parts'.[30] It is an assumption expressed as late as the twentieth century, and even by E. M. Forster (see ch. 3). Henry Rider Haggard's
King Solomon's Mines associates the garden with the heroic English
nation, noting that: 'You can never get your Zulu to take much
interest in gardening. It is a peaceful art, and peaceful arts are not in
his line.'[31]

Addison may celebrate the garden as a site of rest, but it is more
often identified in relation to Englishness with the simple life of honest hard work. Gardening presents the gardener – like Adam and
Eve – in the role of overseer and controller of the potentially wild. In
Wordsworth's 'Tintern Abbey', we find the island state described as
garden, 'wild' connoting a safely bounded and controlled landscape:

> Once again I see
> These hedge-rows, hardly hedge-rows, little lines
> Of sportive wood run wild: these pastoral farms,
> Green to the very door[.] (ll. 14–17)[32]

Gardening involves work, a correlation that, as outlined by Carlyle
in his *Past and Present* of 1843, also enables access to a higher reality: 'For there is a perennial nobleness, and even sacredness, in Work
[. . .] Work, never so Mammonish, mean, is in communication with
Nature; the real desire to get Work done will itself lead one more and
more to truth, to Nature's appointments and regulations, which are
truth' (p. 244).

Into the Victorian period, George Eliot's and Thomas Hardy's
novels of the literary pastoral (as opposed to the cityscapes of Dickens
or Trollope) are ubiquitously cited as representatives of Englishness.
Patrick Parrinder cites Amos Barton's description of 'commonplace
people' as having 'a pathos in their very insignificance' to assert that
Eliot's 'discovery of complexity in simplicity is part of the democra-
tization of the English novel'.[33] But Eliot also underlines the importance of simplicity, and especially the simple life, to the vivacity of
Englishness in many of her novels. In *Adam Bede*, Eliot undercuts an
aristocratic sense of Englishness, overlaying it with the simple,
straightforward, common-sense figure of Adam Bede. Arthur
Donnithorne, heir to the estate, is a strange mixture of the altruistic

and the self-absorbed. At the opening of chapter 12, Eliot presents Arthur in a narcissistic stance before a mirror, underlining the egoism in this otherwise well-meaning English gentleman who contemplates 'his well-looking British person reflected in the old-fashioned mirror'. Pondering his entanglement with Hetty, Arthur focuses never on her but, as the mirror suggests, only on himself. Reflecting on his own character, he compliments himself in thinking that 'candour was one of his favourite virtues', that he identifies as a fundamental characteristic of the 'British person'. The terminology moves from British to English in his vision of a specific, aristocratic, future. His imaginings

> when he should come into the estate, were made up of a prosperous, contented tenantry, adoring their landlord, who would be the model of an English gentleman – mansion in the first-rate order, all elegance and high taste – jolly housekeeping – finest stud in Loamshire – purse open to all public objects.

Based in the Jonsonian myth of the elegant, tasteful, generous English gentleman, this view of Arthur is poignantly contrasted with a scene of Adam in which Eliot outlines for us the form of the true English gentleman. We find Adam in chapter 38 on his way to see Dinah with a disinterested magnanimity free from Arthur's self-absorption. As he walks the roads he is 'picturing the benefits that might come from the exertion of a single country gentleman' – echoing Arthur's previous imaginings – which for Adam consist of 'getting the roads made good in his own district', a sensible and practical approach to the land. It is here that we are given an overview of Adam's qualities: he 'had a devout mind, though he was perhaps rather impatient of devout words, and his tenderness lay very close to his reverence'. Here, it is a dislike of 'devout words', of the verbal elaboration of virtue, as distinct from the practicality of piety that Adam embodies. It is his application that sets him as heroically English in the very chapter, entitled 'The Quest', that implicates him as a knight: 'But after feeling had welled up and poured itself out in this way, busy thought would come back with the greater vigour; and this morning it was intent on schemes[. . .]'. Although he has 'the blood of the peasant in his veins' (ch. 16), Adam thinks in the way the English gentleman should: in a straightforward, practical way, unencumbered by merely decorative talk. It is the humble, hard-working and straight-talking Adam Bede who is England's true son. Dinah Morris's marriage to Adam rather than his brother Seth, further specifies Adam's grounded, masculine, earthy practicality as superior to that of his more sensitive, Methodist brother.

Parrinder notes, in his *Nation and Novel*, Dorothea Brooke's Puritan character, a 'hereditary strain of Puritan energy', and even draws attention to her plain dress and what Eliot calls her 'Puritanic toleration', so trying to her sister as they try on their mother's jewels (Parrinder, p. 259). But it is Dorothea's attitude to aesthetics, her taste, that demonstrates the legacy of the aesthetic of simplicity. Dorothea's beauty, portrayed at the opening of Eliot's *Middlemarch,* demonstrates to the observant reader her value as someone of distinguished taste, the quintessence of virtue. The novel opens: 'Miss Brooke had that kind of beauty which seems to be thrown into relief by poor dress.' 'Poor' is soon qualified by the more specific term 'plain', a term used twice within the first paragraph ('plain garments' and 'plain dressing'). Dorothea stands as a representative of the perfect English type within Eliot's 'provincial life' and against the tastelessly ostentatious preferences of the lower classes. Eliot explains that 'young women of such birth, living in a quiet country-house, and attending a village church hardly larger than a parlor, naturally regarded frippery as the ambition of a huckster's daughter'. As part of a fashionable 'well-bred economy' which necessitates purchases 'more distinctive of rank', plainness is a marker of the English higher classes, against the tastelessness of the 'huckster', a nomenclature that, with its build-up of fricatives, even seems itself overly ornamented and ugly. In Eliot's use of 'naturally' there is the suggestion of irony; for the young women in question are presented as the products of society and their natural inclination the results of 'breeding'. Eliot identifies Dorothea's status as the source of her taste: 'Such reasons would have been enough to account for plain dress, quite apart from religious feeling', she insists. The 'huckster' is simple, it seems, only in terms of impoverishment, but the higher ranks embrace a different order of simplicity to set themselves apart: the lower and higher classes are thereby brought together in a similar, but not identical, aesthetic that takes its value from each class's discreet quality of simplicity. It is precisely because Dorothea is drawn, albeit unconsciously, to the markers of her own rank and repulsed by the vulgar signs of ambition (frippery) – impulses that are strong despite her unquestionable 'religious feeling' – that renders the full strength of such aesthetics: they can be felt and enacted by a range of religious or non-religious sensibilities.

Dorothea's plain clothes render her as a living and carnal example of Scripture, but more because of the impression she gives than because of her spiritual state:

> her stature and bearing seemed to gain the more dignity from her plain garments, which by the side of provincial fashion gave her the impressiveness of a fine quotation from the Bible, – or from one of our elder poets, – in a paragraph of to-day's newspaper.

Dorothea is likened to the Bible, which, in its very association, or more accurately its easy substitution, with 'one of our elder poets' (perhaps, Wordsworth, one infers, a writer frequently regarded in biblical terms), is an aesthetic comparison: she is impressive, a fine quotation. It is her style that gestures towards something intangibly, and yet unquestionably, superior. She is for provincial fashion what the Bible or Wordsworth is for the everyday, ordinary, writing of the newspaper. She is the embodied heritage of the Bible's influence upon the English individual: a residue of an aesthetic impressiveness that has little doctrinal specificity. Dorothea's aesthetic is not only a personal idiosyncrasy (although to some degree its specific articulation in Dorothea is an eccentric version), it marks her as representative of the English upper classes. Simplicity functions here as a pointer to the reader of Dorothea's superiority, of the distinction of her soul as much as Rosamond's 'frippery' and deceitful use of aesthetics are markers of her spiritual dearth. As part of a novel valued for its depiction of an Englishness both marginal and representative, simplicity is a key factor in Eliot's semiology.

The scene in which Dorothea and Celia try on their mother's jewellery adds to Dorothea's characterization as tasteful (already deftly rendered in the novel's opening), a hermeneutic transparency. It also underlines the priority of aesthetics for simplicity, not just for Dorothea or Eliot, but for how simplicity – as a term that straddles conceptual and aesthetic realms – works. Their mother's jewels are repeatedly rendered as 'ornaments' and 'trinkets', emphasizing their superfluous nature in opposition to Dorothea's plain garments. Dorothea demonstrates her religious seriousness in her rejection of a pearl and diamond crucifix: 'A cross is the last thing I would wear as a trinket' (ch. 1), she states, yet professes a liberality towards her sister's wearing of it as more fitting to her soul's 'complexion'. Directly after she articulates her dismissal of the jewellery wholesale, she is drawn to some emeralds newly irradiated by sunlight. Their colour, she notes, 'seem to penetrate one, like scent'. Although Eliot does not use the term simple in this passage, Dorothea's rationalization of her acceptance of a 'trinket' is dependent upon the binary previously set up between 'frippery' (to which ornament and trinket are associated) and 'plain'. Simplicity is implicated in Dorothea's rationalization of her attraction to the emeralds through its hermeneutic relation, transparency. What touches Dorothea about the gem is the resonance of transparency in both aesthetic and transcendent senses ('seem to penetrate one') as she rationalizes her response in biblical terms: 'I suppose that is the reason why gems are used as spiritual emblems in the Revelation of St John. They look like fragments of heaven.' Gems are valued by Dorothea because they speak to her of the imminence of divine revelation – of the nearness of the divine and of the clarity of sight of the prophet (and by inference, the theophany of the prophetic book, Revelation, and its canonical whole, the Bible). Dorothea is drawn to the ornamental trinkets not for their beauty but because they become a sign – and not just any sign, but one within a biblical or heavenly semiology. As 'fragments of heaven', they not only point to the divine, but render divinity present.

Yet again, what is dominant here is not the theological but the aesthetic. As Eliot notes, Dorothea in this speech 'was trying to justify her delight in the colours by merging them with her mystic religious joy'. Eliot suggests that it is Dorothea's mysticism, a spiritual joy as clouded and unspecific as her aesthetic delight, that allows her to make such rationalizations. It is as though, in her grasping for a defence of her newly found sensual pleasure, she plucks the biblical reference from the recesses of her mind. But Dorothea's invocation of the gems of St. John's revelation is no fluffy mystical response, but instead the specific interpretation of the clarity and penetrating, oracular, qualities of the gemstone as suggestive of transcendent revelation. Dorothea recognizes the spiritual significance of the gems as much as she experiences it as pleasurable. To say that Dorothea 'was trying to justify her delight' is not necessarily to give Dorothea's rational capacities too much onus here – it is clear that her efforts of rationalization are so deep-grained that they function instinctually. It is true that Dorothea is a character who yearns to see more clearly and who is desperate for prophetic vision and thereby more sensitive to the aesthetics of transparency than other characters. That Dorothea's movement from transparency to revelation is so easy, however, is suggestive of a wider cultural and social instinct that overlaps the two qualities. The aesthetics of transparency, it seems, are already morally, and potentially spiritually, encumbered.

Dorothea wears plain clothes and is drawn to heavenly gems because she is a discerning reader. Yet Dorothea is, throughout the novel, a strange mixture of being a deceived and penetrating reader. Pre-empting her later misreading of her own needs regarding marriage and the character of Casaubon, Eliot presents to us in this chapter at least a Dorothea who is not entirely self-aware, who is erratic. Dorothea's rejection, then partial acceptance, of the jewels is for Celia 'inconsistent' and strongly contrasts with Celia's own 'common sense' reflection: 'I am sure [. . .] that the wearing of a necklace will not interfere with my prayers.' But Dorothea is someone over whom 'there darted now and then a keen discernment', with the qualifier that it 'was not without a scorching quality'. Her potentially blistering discrimination is nonetheless belied by a lack of self-reflection that is telling of the force of the mythologies of religion in her life. Mythologies, yet again, are shown to be resilient despite any contradicting evidence. Dorothea may be flawed throughout the novel, but our first view of her in her plain garments makes her the skillful interpreter and paragon of taste that the reader must accept her as in order to sympathize with her throughout the epic tale.

Like Spenser's Redcrosse, Dorothea's quest in the novel includes learning to read. Eliot paints her as moving from her limited life, in which she can misread the blinkered Casaubon as noble, to an enlarged sympathy. Her sympathy and discernment are entwined, as in her penetrating understanding of Rosamond, who she nevertheless reaches out to (ch. 81). In Eliot, then, simplicity and sympathy are entwined: it is Rosamond's and Hetty's 'frippery' that stunt their sympathy, that encourages their self-involvement. As the trope of the web in *Middlemarch* demonstrates, recognizing one's own sociality is essential to authentic living for Eliot, and it is frippery that dulls the individual to their social sphere. Eliot's characters that represent the virtues of simplicity – Dorothea, Adam Bede, Dinah Morris – are those that are also the most feelingly, yet practically, sympathetic to the needs of others. Dorothea demonstrates a Ruskinian sympathy in her reaction to the revelatory emeralds. After deciding to take the emeralds as her own, she comments: 'Yet what miserable men find such things, and work at them, and sell them!'. She cannot remain in a world of divine contemplation but tumbles back to earth and its abrasive realities. She rejects aesthetics that ignore human suffering, such as her uncle's paintings of quaint rusticity (that itself echoes the sentiments of the opening chapter of *Mill on the Floss*). Her fervent attention to the workers' cottages sets her as someone who materializes her sympathy, and who reads materiality sympathetically. Like Spenser's Redcrosse, Dorothea becomes a redeemed reader.

Another novel of the 'provinces', Thomas Hardy's *Far From the Madding Crowd*, presents an Edenic England. Hardy's influence on ongoing mythologies of Englishness is testified by Gervais who states that 'no writer of the period has shaped, and shapes, our idea of England more than Hardy' (p. 22). An unsigned review in *Saturday Review*, 9 January 1875 praises his choice of 'simple and natural subjects' but advises Hardy to 'cultivate simplicity of diction' demonstrating both Hardy's and his critics' prioritizing of simplicity.[34] Havelock Ellis praises Hardy for his women's 'subtle simplicity', which makes them 'half ethereal and half homely'. He goes on: 'They are fascinating to us at once, and irresistibly, because they are simple by nature and so involved by circumstance' (Cox, *Hardy's Critical Heritage*, p. 117). Ellis's 'at once' suggests the transparency, the access for the reader, bound up in simplicity.

It is the character of Gabriel Oak who, for Hardy, epitomizes simplicity in its rural superiority. Colls writes in his *Identity of England* that Gabriel's name is well chosen: 'The oak was a slow grower – a tree that declared confidence in the continuity of things' (pp. 206–7). If we turn to Hardy's poem 'Domicillium' we find a specific reference to the oak as a symbol of the continuance of the past into the present:

An oak uprises, springing from a seed
Dropped by some bird a hundred years ago.

At this point the poem changes its focus from a garden to the speaker's grandmother, from the present to the past, with the segue: 'In days bygone –/ Long gone – my father's mother . . . ', underlining the heritage present in the landscape. Past and present as well as people and landscape are entwined (the poem's pun 'hardy flowers' in the description of the garden places the poet in nature). Gabriel Oak communicates just such a heritage, presenting an ancient, almost legendary figure, who becomes destitute when his flock of sheep tragically veer off a cliff edge.

Gabriel is the ultimate reader: he correctly reads the signs of an oncoming storm and saves Bathsheba's livelihood. Indeed, nature speaks to him. In the form of a toad crossing his path, he receives a 'direct message from the Great Mother', deified nature. His finding a slug in his home is another clue, described as 'Nature's second way of hinting to him'. For Oak alone, 'Every voice in nature was unanimous in bespeaking change' (ch. 36). His exemplary reading of landscape is suggested in the extent of his sight under the flash of lightning (naturally imbued vision): 'Gabriel from his elevated position could see over the landscape at least half-a-dozen miles in front. Every hedge, bush, and tree, was distinct as in a line engraving' (ch. 37). Set above his peers, as an angelic figure Gabriel is also the messenger of the gods, a prophetic figure who foresees danger, who reads the signs of the times and brings salvation. His organic relation to nature makes it transparent to him. The English landscape, not the individual soul, is again the site of divine revelation.

Gabriel's nemesis Sergeant Troy is incapable of reading or nurturing the landscape that is his responsibility. Ian Ousby suggests that his military uniform signifies his displacement from the English countryside. The glaring scarlet 'cavalry tunic is the epitome of his shallow superficiality, his lack of inherence in the landscape and the rural community'.[35] Troy, disjointed from nature, undermines the simple life in his rhetoric of seduction. He leads the workers into a catatonic drunkenness through verbal persuasion, insisting 'drinking should be the bond of their union' (ch. 36), making them incapable of saving the grain that is at risk in the storm. He is dangerously deceptive in his luring of Bathsheba (and it seems also himself). Ousby has suggested Troy's naming of Bathsheba as 'Queen of the Corn-market' is an echo of the Miltonic Satan's 'Empress of this fair world', naming the scene 'a provincial mock-heroic version of Satan's apotheosis'.[36] He has also noted Bathsheba's depiction as an Eve figure.[37] In transposing Satan's seduction of Eve to the 'edge of the haymead', and into the figures of Troy and Bathsheba, Hardy repeats Milton's suspicion of rhetoric, reworking his construction of simplicity and continuing its associations with transparency. In the scene, likened to the devil through reference to Tophet, Troy is a self-proclaimed 'idolater', profane and blasphemous, whose linguistic skill entices

Bathsheba. The danger Troy presents is hinted at in Bathsheba's association of his rhetorical skill with his swordsmanship, in which pleasure is conflated with harm: 'If you can only fight half as winningly as you talk, you are able to make a pleasure of a bayonet wound!' This is indeed what happens as Troy's seduction of Bathsheba is inevitably destructive. Troy's depiction here only works to underscore Gabriel's value as a straightforward and thoroughly rural, true Englishman.

The Reformation nexus of simplicity's signifieds of moral and hermeneutic transparency and its concomitants rationality and self-control are mapped onto the English landscape and its exemplary inhabitants in eighteenth- and nineteenth-century literature. Increasingly divorced from Protestant rhetoric, simplicity as an aesthetic, in visual terms and as delineated in the simple countryside, continues as the locus of the salvific.

CHAPTER THREE

CONTEMPORARY ENGLISHNESS AND THE PROTESTANT AESTHETIC

When Prime Minister John Major wanted to convince his party of his loyalty to British sovereignty in his speech to the Conservative Group for Europe, 22 April 1993, he invoked an image of England that would, he claimed, persist for generations. In fifty years,

> Britain will still be the country of long shadows on county grounds, warm beer, invincible green suburbs, dog lovers and pools fillers and – as George Orwell said – 'old maids biking to Holy Communion through the morning mist'.

Major presents an England defined by its landscape – albeit a contained *suburban* green landscape of dog walking, cricket, paddling pools and morning mist – and by its literary past. Likened by Paxman to Stanley Baldwin's series of idealistic talks of the 1920s (*The English*, p. 142), Major's speech is representative of attempts to invoke an unchanging England, a timelessness that depends upon the landscape's and literature's seemingly eternal qualities. Scruton too turns to cricket, that for him displays

> the reticent and understated character of the English ideal: white flannels too clean and pure to suggest physical exertion, long moments of silence and stillness, stifled murmurs of emotion should anything out of the ordinary occur and the occasional burst of subdued applause. (pp. 14–15)

Scruton portrays in the cricket scene the impulse of simplicity: the pared down aesthetics ('white flannels'), sound ('silence and still-ness') and emotion ('stifled murmurs') convey a clean, pure, con-trolled and reserved Englishman. A similar impulse dominates his list of English characteristics: 'gentleness, firmness, honesty, toler-ance, "grist", the stiff upper lip and the spirit of fair play' (p. 21). Ian Baucom outlines in his fascinating study, *Out of Place*, that 'English-ness has consistently been defined through appeals to the identity-endowing properties of place' (p. 4), and cites the cricket field as such a quintessentially English site. The practice of situating English character in the landscape, he claims, 'serves a disciplinary and nos-talgic discourse on English national identity by making the past visible by rendering it present, by acting as what Pierre Nora calls a *lieu de memoire* that purports to testify to the nation's essential continuity across time' (pp. 4–5). As Nora notes, such sites act 'to stop time, to block the work of forgetting', asserting instead a 'will to remember'.[1] Pertaining to geographical place, Nora's claims are equally applicable to the places of literature. Both the material landscape and literary images of England are the perfect sites for English mythologies, for making present the past, for encouraging a 'will to remember', as they communicate an imagined identity, an ideal, while appearing to be nothing more than the concrete site of everyday life.

This chapter will consider the depictions of such a timeless Eng-lishness that depend upon the situating of English character within a seemingly unchanging, ideal English landscape and literature. Its first half will look to writings that figure English simplicity in the landscape, providing a concrete foundation for English character. I offer a detailed reading of Edward Thomas's *Heart of England* (1907), and refer to E. M. Forster's *Howard's End* (1910), perhaps one of the most celebrated depictions of an ideal England. Both works present simplicity as imbued in a landscape that demonstrates its continued connections with simplicity: transparency, honesty and qualities of self-control. While Englishness is indirectly expressed in writings on the landscape, writers in the early twentieth century also started to reflect more explicitly on national identity. The second half of the chapter turns to these writings that deal explicitly with English charac-ter. Countering Kumar's view that it is only in the end of the nineteenth century that writers 'for the first time began an inquiry into the char-acter of the English people as a nation' (*The Making of English National*

Identity, p. 224, we saw in the last chapter earlier instances), Parrinder identifies instead at this point a 'greater self-consciousness than ever before, but also in an increasingly sceptical and critical spirit' (p. 291). In these writings, a 'greater self-consciousness' is apparent, but an indirect mode of writing is still in force in which an intuitive response to the aesthetics of Englishness results in vague, and often seemingly contradictory, portraits of national character. The English are rational, but also intuitive, controlled, emotionally reserved and above all, exemplary. Orwell will be a principal focus and considered primarily in relation to his short work, *The English People* (1947), which in distinction to the class-based and nuanced arguments of *The Lion and the Unicorn* presents the more stable and nostalgic sense of the 'Orwellian England' (see p. 117) that he is associated with.

In all of these works Protestantism is, at best, a relic of English moral character, not a living religion. Indeed, Orwell was notoriously atheistic. Orwell presents 'puritanism' as a controlling sentiment, defined 'in the looser sense in which the word is generally used (that is, prudishness, asceticism, the "kill-joy" spirit)' as something 'forced upon the working class by the class of small traders and manufacturers immediately above them' (*English People*, p. 16). He dismisses a link between 'puritanism' and historical religious Puritanism, or Calvinism as he calls it, asserting that this 'dismal theology' 'never popularised itself in England as it did for a while in Wales and Scotland' (p. 16). Orwell is correct insofar as Calvinism per se did not endure in such strong forms in England as it did in Wales and Scotland, but as we have seen in Chapter One, Calvin's writings were influential on popular forms of Protestantism (and not just Puritanism) in the early modern period. Yet, Orwell's distancing of puritan character traits from religion is typical of the ways in which Protestantism or the Reformation are commonly invoked as shapers of Englishness, but are separated into, on the one hand, a national, legal, democratic and secular 'core' and, on the other, its religious clothing, as we saw with Greenfeld (see p. 6). Writers are often averse to religious sentiment, transposing Reformation impulses into more 'English' concepts. John Fowles, for example, describes Protestantism as 'a function of our concept of the Just Outlaw', pressing Protestantism into a sense of rebellion so that 'socialism is a product of dissent expressing itself through reform, Chartism, Bradlaughism, trade unionism and the rest' (p. 160). For Fowles, England's Protestant history becomes one of just resistance, separate from any overtly religious element. Any sense of a doctrinal continuance in Protestantism is lacking in writings on Englishness, although its most tenacious doctrine, that of the English as the chosen people, has been largely manifest in the popularity of Parry's popularizing of Blake's poem in his hymn 'Jerusalem'. Orwell and his contemporaries – the repository of ideals of Englishness – can be considered as carrying forward Protestant principles only in their heralding of the aesthetic and principle of simplicity.

*   *   *

The English landscape is both tangibly real and ideally unreal. As Paxman outlines, the ideal is superimposed upon the actual:

> In the collective unconscious [. . .] there exists another England. It is not the country in which the English actually live, but the place they *imagine they are in*. It touches the reality they see around them at various points, but it is something ideal[.] (p. 144)

Although the terms British and English are often treated as synonymous – not least in Orwell's works – Englishness in such nostalgic writings is distanced from political realities (Britishness) and identified as a longstanding cultural identity. As John Fowles explains, Britishness is 'a recent façade clapped on a much older building' (p. 154) and he articulates the difference as 'the split in the English mind between the Green England and the Red-white-and-blue Britain' (pp. 155–6). Political realities are sidelined in the pursuit of an unsullied Green England.

Because the ideal England, as Paxman notes, is not the one in which 'the English actually live', assertions of England as urban, modern and modernizing ignore the necessary disparity between reality and myth. Peter Mandler interrogates the rural impulse of English sentiment and argues convincingly that the English characteristics of 'pragmatism, puritanism and utilitarianism', 'if anything cast the English as more naturally urban and egalitarian' ('Against Englishness', p. 155). Mandler argues that the 'rural-nostalgic vision of "Englishness" remained the province of impassioned and highly articulate but fairly marginal artistic groups', for example in works by Arnold and Ruskin (p. 170) and that even after the wars the emphasis was on a progressive, suburban identity, that embraced aspirations for the 'technological, the timely and the up-to-the-minute'

(p. 175). For Mandler, rural nostalgia 'reflects more than most historical writing the agenda of the present rather than the story of the past' (p. 175). In trying to map myths to empirical historical evidence, Mandler misses the point of the tenacity of myths and their disjunction from the facts of reality. Such mythologies can only ever be partially true and distributed unevenly across the population with often elite or minority expression. Myths configured in such conceptual terms depend heavily on a set of ideal images that bestow iconographic importance. Scruton, indeed, defends an English ideal by asserting a clear literary heritage. The literature from the Second World War itself

> drew upon the works of such real and self-imagined countrymen as Richard Jefferies, W. D. Hudson and H. J. Massingham; it took up the themes of Lady Eve Balfour and the Soil Association (still active today in defence of organic farming); it harked back to Ruskin and the pre-Raphaelites, and further to the Lakeland poets and the idylls of Shakespeare. It achieved influential but soggy embodiment in the post-First-World-War speeches of Prime Minister Stanley Baldwin. (p. 40)

In such literary works is found a repository of positive images of English identity, contained in a seemingly timeless and simple landscape and in characteristics of honesty, discernment, straightforwardness and self-possession.

The desire for continuity in England's identity demands an elision of empirical evidence. In his *The English People*, Orwell begins by noting the disjunction between past and present-day representations of the English. He compares the England depicted in Hogarth's prints, in which the English seemingly 'spent their time in an almost unending round of fighting, whoring, drunkenness, and bull-baiting', and the contrasting world of the 'gentle-mannered, undemonstrative, law-abiding English of to-day' (p. 12). He recognizes the difficulty of drawing an historical trajectory that he is nonetheless committed to:

> This is one of those questions, like the freedom of the will or the identity of the individual, in which all the arguments are on one side and instinctive knowledge is on the other. It is not easy to discover the connecting thread that runs through English life from

the sixteenth century onwards, but all English people who bother about such subjects feel that it exists. (p. 12)

There is a desire, in other words, to connect with the past and to prioritize an enduring, stable, identification. In *The Lion and the Unicorn* he argues that England is 'continuous, it stretches into the future and the past, there is something in it that persists, as in a living creature'.[2] While recognizing 'the diversity of it, the chaos!' (p. 252), Orwell is nonetheless committed, counterintuitively, to continuity. He speaks from common sense: 'in fact anyone able to use his eyes knows that the average of human behaviour differs enormously from country to country' and goes on: 'there *is* something distinctive and recognizable in English civilization' (p. 252).

Orwell's complex, and even contradictory, political writings become conservative mythology as snapshots of his vision of England are put to work to naturalize the historical. Orwell is made contemporary and his writings have become an unarguable locus for discussions of Englishness even though the context of his 'old maids' is a list of seemingly incompatible images of England that for him present 'the diversity of it, the chaos!' (p. 252). This Orwellian England is the green and pleasant Englishness that Scruton appeals to and which he claims he has caught merely a glimpse of through his contact with older generations. Following the gaze of one of his adored teachers, Scruton sees the ideal as 'a consecrated isle in the lake of forgetting, where the God of the English still strode through an imaginary Eden, admiring His works' (p. 32). Recognizably prelapsarian, for Scruton England is 'first and foremost, the countryside' (p. 39), innocent and homely, yet Edenic and paradisiacal. Parry's hymn of this 'green and pleasant *land*' (Scruton's emphasis) transformed, he claims, the 'violent form' of seventeenth-century Puritanism – England as a New Israel manifested in the civil war – into the anthem of the brass band movement, the Suffragettes and the Women's Institute, which for Scruton demonstrates the innocence of the English attachment to landscape: 'What had begun as the martial call to arms, threatening the overthrow of everything, ended, in a typically English manner, as a choral anthem for ladies' (p. 20). That the 'tribal and religious' is converted to the domesticated only proves to Scruton the harmlessness of English mythologies (rather than the extent of ideological assent). He asserts 'the inimitable sense of England as a society rooted in a landscape, growing from topography and climate under the protection of a unique religion and law'. He paints a picture of Englishness in which character finds a material basis in land and climate, with religion and law acting as knightly defenders. But it is not just religion and law, but literature that must act as chivalrous protector. Land is dependent upon literary 'enchantment', Scruton insists, demonstrating the foundational status of literature to his sense of England. He finds his England in 'Shakespeare's Arden, in Milton's Eden, in Gray's Elegy, in the poetry of John Clare, in the novels of Fielding, in Blake's lyrics and mystical writings and – pre-eminently – in the *Prelude* of Wordsworth' and asserts the sublimation of landscape by Hardy, Hopkins, Lawrence and Eliot's *Four Quartets*. These writers, he claims, reach through landscape to the truth of things: 'to discover another order, a hidden order, which had been overlayed [sic] by history but which was, nevertheless, the true meaning of that history and the deep-down explanation of our being here' (p. 41). Writer and landscape work in a mutual relationship, the writer as the elect, accessing the transcendence of England's landscape for the English who need the penetrating, prophetic, redeemed sight of their writers. Although commonly identified as a Romantic construction, in landscape description it is often the Miltonic landscape that is invoked, for example in Christine Berberich's 'pre-lapsarian, unspoilt Arcadian idyll'.[3] The landscape is Edenic, transcendent and eternal. It represents access to truth and the divine in a way that other mediations, such as language, are not capable of.

The prevalence of such conservative configurations of Englishness is apparent in the popularity of the quarterly magazine *This England*, published since 1967 in Cheltenham. As Paxman explains, this 'non-U' (middle-class) publication outsells the combined subscription of *New Statesman*, *Tatler*, the *Spectator* and *Country Life* (pp. 77–8). In such popular expressions, England becomes the Eden of the simple, rustic life; a life depicted in a magazine that may be a far cry from the places in which its readers 'actually live' (many subscribers are ex-pats in foreign lands). As Rebecca Scutt and Alastair Bonnett outline in their analysis of *This England* (among similar publications), 'the rural became a simple place, a place steeped in timeless traditions and values'.[4] Scutt and Bonnett demonstrate how situating Englishness in such a 'simple place' also implicitly simplifies English identity: 'by locating "the spirit of England", "enchanting

England" and "this England" in a mythically perfect vision of a past rural life, any *explicit* connection between the countryside (and so Englishness) and middle-class Whiteness can be avoided' (p. 23). The set of English characteristics – for example Scruton's 'gentleness, firmness, honesty, tolerance, "grist", the stiff upper lip and the spirit of fair play' – are uncomplicated by the reality of different cultures. The now ideal landscape and its narrowly defined ideal inhabitants are also overlaid with, and sustained by, literary mythologies.

Even Orwell, despite the political complexity of his writing, presents an auratic landscape, positing its uniquely recuperative effects. In *The Lion and the Unicorn* he asserts:

> When you come back to England from any foreign country, you have immediately the sensation of breathing a different air. (p. 252)

The image is the central motif in his novel *Coming up for Air*. The protagonist, George Bowling (whose initials, G. B. make him a representative Brit, but also clearly English), while driving on a work errand pulls over to pick flowers in a field: 'I felt I'd got to get out and have a smell at the spring air, and perhaps even pick a few primroses if there was nobody coming'. Bowling situates the recuperative air in a wider, ideal landscape:

> I hitched my hat back a bit to get the kind of balmy feeling of the air against my forehead. The grass under the hedge was full of primroses. Just inside the gate a tramp or somebody had left the remains of a fire. A little pile of white embers, and a wisp of smoke still oozing out of them. Further along there was a little bit of pool, covered over with duck-weed. The field was winter wheat. It sloped up sharply, and then there was a fall of chalk and a little beech spinney. A kind of mist of young leaves on the trees. And utter stillness everywhere.[5]

It is in this still, simple scene that Bowling in a rare instance feels '*happy*' and that 'life was worth living'. Even a tramp's fire is subsumed within the ideal as it evokes for Bowling the land's hospitality. The English are nurtured and characterized by their land. Their love of 'flowers, gardening and "nature"', he argues, is ideological: 'a part of their vague aspiration towards an agricultural life' (*English People*, p. 46). It is a recourse to the simple life.

EDWARD THOMAS'S AND E. M. FORSTER'S
SIMPLE LANDSCAPE

Edward Thomas was a poet and defender of patriotic love for the English countryside that was for him the source of a tranquility within hectic modernity. Michael Kirkham sees in Thomas the same nostalgia that is often identified in other wartime writers such as Evelyn Waugh: 'As the reality of England faded, the nearer it seemed to approach extinction, the more urgently was Thomas spurred to the imaginative realization of an ideal England'.[6] This ideal England in Thomas's words 'offers symbols of peace, security and everlasting-ness', epitomized in the 'long, starry herbage', the 'wide meadows where the cows wander half a mile an hour'.[7] Although often writing from a liminal site between Wales and England (like Wordsworth and his Wye Valley poetry), he presents the simplicity of the specifically English countryside in his prose *Heart of England* (1906), in which the narration of a walk from the city, through the countryside to the sea, performs the move from centre to boundary. Thomas infers from the landscape the qualities of honesty, justice and purity. The Watercress man, that the protagonist of the book meets on his walk, points to the unmediated purity of the landscape:

> literature does not believe in or understand the honest life, bound up with the seasons and beauty which is expressed by that simple scene. See, there, equal laws, harmony, aims, unspotted by the world, not fearing nor loving kings. Any thoughtful man living in a scene like that would be wiser, and it would be impossible for him to err. (p. 14)

The honest life is identified in the 'simple scene', simplicity signify-ing fairness ('equal laws'), temperance ('harmony'), revelation (bestowing wisdom, it seems by osmosis, to those who live in it), rationality and purity (inhabitants are wise and, like Wordsworth's picnickers, cannot 'err'). Landscape unmediated even by literature (a deprecatory reflection by the poet Thomas) is revelatory. The Watercress man who utters these words is indeed the archetype of the 'thoughtful man living in' the landscape, bound up with its 'seasons and beauty', earning his living from the seasonal fecundity of landscape – watercress and flowers – and from the reflection of its beauty in his paintings.

The natural world, in its simplicity, is the site of authentic knowledge throughout the book. Thomas depicts the transformation of English countryside specifically in terms of a paradise lost, imbuing nature with an Edenic quality and human artifice as marring an originally pure creation. In his view of the urbanized landscape, 'Ivied elm trunks lay about with scaffold poles, uprooted shrubs were mingled with bricks, mortar with turf, shining baths and sinks and rusty fire grates with dead thistles and thorns.' As the sentence progresses the natural world gives way to the linguistic priority of the man-made, as clauses open at first with elm and shrubs, but then with mortar, shining baths and fire grates, a progression that echoes the overtaking of the landscape by the artificial. He goes on:

> Here and there a man in a silk hat or a little girl with neat ankles and high brown boots stepped amidst the deeply rutted mud. An artist who wished to depict the Fall and some sympathy with it in the face of a ruined Eden might have had little to do but copy an acre of the surviving fields. (p. 4)

The English countryside becomes auratic and divine as Thomas depicts the scene of building as a reliving of the moment of the Fall – of the innocent moving towards corruption. Nature maintains the potential to redeem the landscape, as he describes a dense, obscuring rain that 'formed a mist and a veil over the skeletons round about' obscuring the scaffolding, and as such 'the trees were back in Eden again. They were as before in their dim, stately companies' (p. 6). Thomas likens the countryside to the newly fallen Adam and Eve, its naked authentic body now covered with the clothing of urbanity. As nudity continues as a sign of the prelapsarian, of innocence and authenticity, so landscape retains its purity. Even in the urban London landscape, at night the hills become apparent in the cadence of the ground: 'in the night we see them as if the streets did not exist' (p. 8). The naked body of the countryside is discernible beneath the city's cladding. The countryside, the river and hills, like the stars, are beyond the reach of the taint of human interference, presenting instead a pure eternal essence: 'The river ran by, grim, dark and vast, and having been untouched by history, old as hills and stars'. The manmade world of 'alleys, lanes, rises, streets' are like 'Inferno and Purgatorio' until he comes across a signpost, which presents a revelatory, and salvatory, knowledge: 'The sign-post seemed to make all things clear. Like a prophet it rose up, who after an age of darkness says that the path of life and goodness is plain, that he knows it, and that all who follow him will be saved' (p. 10). In the manmade landscape, as in the postlapsarian world itself, is a messenger from God, a prophet and signpost that enables Thomas to know his place and his way. The marred landscape, like the fallen world, contains the potential and even the promise of revelation.

Thomas presents a nostalgia for the 'Golden Age', which the Watercress Man, despite his dismissal of literature, claims is accessed through 'the pastoral poets' (p. 13). Art and landscape have distinct effects upon the individual. Nature, he insists, is beyond human grasping and cannot be painted 'as she is', instead one can only 'aim for suggestion' (p. 13). Nature must be experienced directly, without mediation. As a privileged site of transcendence, any reproduction will at once be an act of mediation and destroy the divine presence. The Watercress Man does not aspire to reproduce correctly, but rather the only claim he makes of his painting is that 'the feeling is there' (p. 13), echoing a Wordsworthian sense of communicating only the emotional experience of epiphany, not revelation itself.

Thomas limns the relation between worker and landscape as organic: rural life imbues people with the land's transcendent associations. The ploughman, along with his plough and three horses, is birthed by the landscape: 'they seem one and glorious' he writes, 'as if the all-breeding earth had just sent them up out of the womb' (p. 21). The ploughman is so earthly that 'the rabbits hardly trouble to hide as he appears'. Richard the ploughman as a named and specific individual is 'swaying with the violent motion of the plough' but 'out of joy and not necessity' (p. 22), unlike others who, Thomas reasons, must be 'turned into a fool by the immense monotony' (p. 23). While expressing a personal repugnance at such a tedious job, Thomas presents Richard instead as 'in league with sun and wind and rain to make odours fume richly from the ancient altar, to keep the earth going in beauty and fruitfulness for still more years'. Richard as ploughman becomes a priest as the landscape is sanctified, a 'holy evening landscape' (p. 31). The description is echoed in Thomas's beech trees that 'extended long priestly branches clothed in leaf, still and curved, to call for silence in the cool, shadowy, crystal air' (p. 48). Landscape and its rural inhabitants enact the role of the priestly mediator between the divine and human, ushering the individual into the presence of God.

The human workers of the land are, like the landscape, transparent and revelatory. The farmer's 'calm, large-featured, sandstone face' is readable as 'filling easily and handsomely with a clear-souled anger and delight' (p. 73). The translucent face, like the soul it reveals, is 'clear', indicating at once an accessibility, openness, authenticity and purity. The clear soul manifests itself, Thomas implies, in the equally pure emotions of anger and delight: a pleasing clarity of emotion and perfect correspondence of self, emotional expression and face. As an archetypal and perfect sign, the ploughman is 'marvellously in harmony with the earth' (p. 73), like Carlyle's 'Man of Practice', he is the perfect conduit of nature's foundational essence. The farmer's clear soul is augmented by his library of theological works including *The Seasons* (by James Thomson, author of *Rule Britannia!*), in which the Miltonic-influenced depiction of the landscape of England is infused with the transcendence of God, a theodicy that in the vein of Milton defends the ways of God to men.[8]

The landscape as accessible and divinely revelatory is also representative of an English sense of universal freedom. The verge that borders the roadside is 'no man's garden'; neither wild nor the property of an individual, it is both cultivated and open. England itself has become a garden. 'Everyone who is nobody sits there', Thomas writes, 'with a special satisfaction', 'secure', and 'free' at least 'to laugh or scoff or wonder or weep at the world' (p. 33). The nobodies of England, with access to the verge, England's democratic garden, can like the rest of the English be the observers of the world around them, inhabiting the privileged position of commentator.

As landscape takes on the revelatory impulse of Protestant theology, so church and landscape blur. In his chapter 'A Decorated Church', the church is 'the same colour as the oak trees round about', making the church like the landscape's human inhabitants, a synecdoche of England. The religious dimension of England (or at least its architectural artefacts), is as aesthetic and ethereal as Englishness itself. Simplicity takes on a revelatory mantle as the church and Christianity both signify only alongside and within the landscape so that the two are indistinguishable. England, not Christianity, is presented in the church's congregation. Diversity is subsumed into type and is portrayed as representative of Englishness itself: 'men and women of all degrees of endurance, chivalry, good intention, uncertain aims, sentimental virtuousness, hypocrisy not dissevered from hardship, vanity, not ignorant of tenderness, hard ambition, the desire to be respected' (p. 44). Seemingly heterogeneous, the church's congregation is instead a spectrum of a specific type. They are expressively diverse, 'they differ each from the rest', Thomas asserts, 'and every one of the gods in all the mythologies must be gladdened or angered at some part of the hymn by the meaning of this or that worshipper: Odin, Apollo, Diana, Astarte, the Cat, the Beetle' (p. 45), but notably not the Christian God. The singing communicates emotion, not doctrine, as 'men and women throw all kinds of strange meaning, heartfelt and present, imaginative, retrospective, expectant, into the vague words of the hymn' (p. 44). Thomas dwells on the sound of the hymn that lingers after the congregation leave, their presence traced in the sonic landscape. His wistful and ephemeral portrait posits an imagined, fairytale giant that cages the singers because 'he loved to hear their voices expressing moods he knew nothing of'. The church becomes other-worldly as it seemingly becomes part of a fable, fantastical and unreal. Consisting of their expressed emotions, the congregants are aligned with the caged bells in the tower 'with mute, patient heads like cows'. As Thomas draws people, livestock, church and bells together, he finally names the bells, and the English, as: 'Solitude, Tranquility, Duty, Harmony, Joy'. These explicit characteristics of Englishness, already implied at various points in his prose, are overwritten by the qualities of simplicity that he repeatedly invokes and that overlay qualities of the Protestant aesthetic of revelatory promise, transparency and rationality.

From the familiar aspect 'In a Farmyard', the narrator becomes lost and experiences threat to the countryside and to England. Thomas invokes satanic imagery from Milton's *Paradise Lost* in the 'snaky-bodied pond', 'older than them all', a 'monstrous, coiled, primaeval thing' (p. 57), which has a 'solitary, dying ash-tree' at its edge. The tree, 'endiademed with woe' (p. 59), invokes Shelley's melancholic poem 'Misery – A Fragment' (l. 10).[9] Thomas also presents a Miltonic depiction of Night, borrowing from *Paradise Lost* book II in which Night and Chaos are rulers of the unformed world and are approached by the lost Satan for directions out of Hell. Positing the lost protagonist of his book as a wandering Satan, Thomas makes explicit the allegorical tendency of landscape as metaphor of

46

England. Thomas invokes at this point in the book a moment of 'error', in its Miltonic sense of wandering, the protagonist's own diversion becoming a fleeting suggestion of spiritual lack. Night is for Milton's Satan the 'eldest of things' (p. 59) and Thomas suggests a primaeval darkness off the track of the well-trodden English landscape that both undercuts his bucolic celebration of England and substantiates it in a specific, cultivated form. The landscape of the pond and ashtree are eerily satanic as Thomas's prose here digresses from the everyday crossing of cows. He transcends to the world of Satan, Chaos and Night, narrating night walks and still evenings, entering the fantastical poetic worlds of Shelley and Milton, to return to the daytime of the prosaic farmyard that one infers is the angelic realm of Edenic innocence.

In E. M. Forster's *Howard's End* (1910) Leonard, like Thomas's protagonist, is sensitive to the significance of the rural landscape.[10] As an autodidact, his literary propensities mark him as a discerning reader. He interprets the rural workers as 'England's hope', organically related to a land in which nature dictates activity so that time is 'ruled, not by a London office, but by the movements of the crops and the sun' (ch. 41). The countryside's simplicity is aligned with the sun, a timeless, natural site of illumination. The sense of nostalgia is clear in the contrast of urban and rural life:

> London was but a foretaste of this nomadic civilization which is altering human nature so profoundly, and throws upon personal relations a stress greater than they have ever borne before. Under cosmopolitanism, if it comes, we shall receive no help from the earth. Trees and meadows and mountains will be only a spectacle, and the binding force that they once exercised on character must be entrusted to Love alone. (ch. 30)

The land is revelatory and Leonard can see 'into the life of things'.[11] On English farms, 'one might see life steadily and see it whole', 'connect without bitterness until all men are brothers' (ch. 30), a perspective that imbues the landscape with revelation and communion.

Parrinder describes Forster's novel as employing 'a kind of nature-mysticism that makes the house seem greater and more meaningful than the families who own and occupy it' (*Nation and Novel*, p. 294). The place is endowed with mystical force only to imbue its inhabitants with equal significance. Forster's assertion of the link between land and character is evident in a school essay he wrote (and won a prize for) entitled 'The Influence of climate and physical conditions upon national character'.[12] Although the content of this article is lost, the title corresponds to the novel's continuation in aesthetic and metaphoric form a scientifically based assumption about the relation between place and character, an association that continued to resonate long after science had refuted such theories.

There is a mysterious connection in which land and people are organically related and for these and later writers, landscape is merely a focus for writing about English character. Colls states with implicit agreement in 2002 that, 'With their lawns folding out onto open land and their little private paths meandering up to personal points of view, the estate gardens of the gentry were said to symbolize English liberties' (p. 204). Priestley reads the English explicitly through the land:

The English mind is like this landscape of hers. There, too, is a haze, rubbing away the hard edges of ideas, softening and blending the hues of passion. Reason is there but it is not all-conquering and triumphant, setting up its pyramids and obelisks or marking out long straight roads down which the battalions of thought must march. (*English Humour*, 8)

Alongside the vagaries of writings on the English landscape is a newly emerging analysis of English character that is similarly indistinct.

SIMPLICITY AND THE ENGLISH CHARACTER

When it comes to rationality, representations of the English seem contradictory. While some writers assert the force of the rational, others remark on the English rejection of cleverness. Sometimes the contradictory positions are expressed by a single writer. For Orwell, rational choice is pre-eminent. He credits the continuity of English character to willful and conscious conformity to an appealing historic type. The mind guides the self. He offers a suggestion in *The English People* that resembles the thrust of his short story, 'Shooting an Elephant': 'Myths which are believed in tend to become true, because they set up a type, or "persona", which the average person will do his best to resemble'. Myths are, in short, wilfully imitated and lived out. In the short story, the young British soldier shoots an elephant purely because it is what is expected of him: it is even a consciously recognized capitulation.[13] While the story's protagonist is unusually self-reflective, the implication of the story is that external expectations are a principal motivator (and may as easily function unconsciously). In positing this act of imitation, Orwell looks to the activities of the English during the Second World War, in order to posit a core of self-control: 'Traditionally the Englishman is phlegmatic, unimaginative, not easily rattled: and since that is what he thinks he ought to be, that is what he tends to become.' If we take the intransitive sense of 'tend' seriously (to carry the sense of natural inclination), then what Orwell is suggesting is that a cognitive model leads to natural disposition. In other words, decision creates inclination. A similar explanation for the working of myths is evident in Colls' analysis – although he considers it a far from successful process. Although lists of 'essential, eternal national characteristics' are 'sociologically illiterate in that they are clearly bound by their specificities of time, place, class, gender and education' (although such elitism is part of the point of mythologies), he goes on to suggest that: 'They may none the less have interesting sociological effects in that some social actors respond to myth – what is real in the mind, can be real in its consequences' (*Identity of England*, pp. 578–9). The English here seem so rational that they can easily conform themselves to their chosen ideal.

Yet Orwell's assertion of conscious imitation is complicated by alternative models of identity elsewhere in his writings that tie into the pervasive claim that the English are not rational, are indeed far from clever, but instead instinctual. Orwell privileges the non-rational in his statement that, for the English, 'their patriotism is largely unconscious' (*The English People*, p. 20). The force of the habitual is expressed in Orwell's *A Clergyman's Daughter*, in which the rituals of church are so emotionally embedded in the daughter's being that she is tied, happily, to the activities of her religion even after she loses her faith. Her inclination works against, not through, conscious affiliation. Orwell's vague theories of continuity seem to belie more fascinating yet less coherent perceptions about human behaviour. George Santayana in *Soliloquies in England* of 1922 suggests a less rational model for the continuity of English identity that portrays the English as an essentially instinctual, not intellectual, people. He locates the core of the self in what he terms the 'inner man', which he enlarges upon as pertaining to 'the hereditary Psyche that breeds the body and its discursive thoughts, craves to exercise ascendancy'.[14] As the term 'hereditary' suggests, the 'inner man' is not, as might first appear, a universal phenomenon, but peculiarly English and traceable, at least implicitly, to Protestantism: 'the true Catholic [. . .] has renounced, or never thought of maintaining, the inner man' (*Soliloquies*, p. 86). Being instinctual – being ruled by the 'inner man' is, then, a peculiarly English and Protestant trait.

Santayana proffers a sense of the Englishman shaped from the inside out, not by rationality, but by instinct, what he calls a man's (and he is talking of men with their 'love and loyalty towards women') 'inner atmosphere, the weather in his soul' (p. 30). This 'internal weather' however, is separate from the body – the Englishman 'resolutely turns in church to the east and recites the Creed (with genuflexions, if he likes genuflexions) without in the least implying that he believes one word of it' (p. 31). Santayana's model separates body and mind as much as rational models, as he sets rationality against instinct. He celebrates, for example, Fielding's 'contrasting preaching and practice, our codes with our actual impulses' (p. 124). He reiterates that 'never is it a precise reason, or purpose, or outer fact that determines him; it is always the atmosphere of his inner man' (p. 31). Santayana goes on to elaborate that this 'weather' is a 'witness to some settled disposition, some ripening inclination for this or that, deeply rooted in his soul. It gives a sense of direction in life which is virtually a code of ethics, and a religion behind a religion' (p. 31). It is not cognitive: 'to say it was the vision of any ideal or allegiance to any principle would be making it far too articulate and abstract'; nor is it linguistic: 'it broods at a much deeper level than language or even thought. It is a mass of dumb instinct and allegiances, the love of a certain quality of life, to be maintained manfully' (p. 31). Priestley reads this 'mass of dumb instincts and allegiances' as something distinctly English, which he expands to explain as 'knowing more or less what we want and what we like but never knowing exactly why, it is perhaps easier for us English to achieve that balance of sympathy and antipathy necessary for the full appreciation of the ludicrous' (*English Humour*, p. 12).

This sense that the English 'know more or less' what they want but 'never know [. . .] exactly why' relates to the repeated rejection of 'cleverness'. Carlyle in the nineteenth century had articulated this sense of the Englishman's character whose speech 'is nine-tenths of it palpable *non*sense', yet the unspoken is trustworthy: 'his inner silent feeling of what is true, what does agree with fact, what is doable and what is not doable' (*Past and Present*, p. 202). From Santayana's identification of 'dumb instincts and allegiances' to Orwell's 'general vagueness'(p.22), the organic functioning of the English is asserted over rationality. The English are instinctual. Priestley observes a commonly iterated judgement of the English in *English Humour*, that they 'do not approach life intellectually [. . .] they are not convinced that the universe can be penetrated by thought' (p. 18). Orwell also sees 'the narrow interests of the average man, the rather low level of English education, the contempt for "highbrows" and the almost general deadness to aesthetic issues' are commonplace but 'serious liabilities' (*English People*, p. 45). Like Priestley, he too celebrates instinct, claiming that the English will 'always prefer instinct to logic, and character to intelligence' (warning nonetheless that 'they must get rid of their downright contempt for "cleverness"', p. 46).

Orwell goes on to unravel the English attitude to 'theories', positing for them instead 'a moral quality which must be vaguely described as decency' (p. 20). The decent thing is instinctually known, but it is also habitual: it is that which is fitting or appropriate. Santayana preempts Orwell to some extent as he posits the English as motivated by taste, that which is instinctually known and habitual. Even religious affiliation, for Santayana, is measured against an instinctual sense of what is unpleasant: 'The Englishman finds that he was born a Christian, and therefore wishes to remain a Christian [. . .] and it is an axiom with him that nothing can be obligatory for a Christian which is unpalatable to an Englishman.' (p. 84).

In Orwell's analysis, the aversion to 'cleverness' belies a belief in the Englishman's natural superiority: 'They have a remarkable readiness to admit that foreigners are more "clever" than themselves, and yet they feel that it would be an outrage against the laws of God and Nature for England to be ruled by foreigners' (*English People*, p. 13). In his acceptance of instinct and character, Orwell communicates a sense in which the English simply 'know' without the recourse to the (perhaps vulgar) mechanics of logic and intelligence. As such the recourse to instinct seen in Santayana, Priestley and Orwell is as much a ratification of the English's discrimination as was an assertion of their rational self-control. Such a sentiment is echoed in Scruton's insistence on the simple affections of simple folk. It is, perhaps, then, a resort to a belief in the Englishman's embodiment of the rational that renders his instinctual judgement superior to logic and intellectual argument. So, despite this ostensible eschewing of intelligence, there is nonetheless recourse to the discerning Englishman.

Such discernment also results in the English prioritization of just-ice. John Fowles asserts that the Englishman's ideal has been 'to live in the justest country in the world' ('On Being English', p. 154). This justice stems from ideals of rationalism, for Fowles, as he explains: 'He is the man too empirical, too independent, too able to compare, to live with injustice and stomach it' (p. 157). The Englishman's sense of justice may be partly moral, but is largely to do with having a heightened perspective, a scientific and rationalist viewpoint from which injustice is seen most clearly. He helpfully differentiates between law and justice: 'We know that justice is always greater than the law and further than the law, further in definition, further in application and further in our history' (p. 162). Here, English legal history (enshrined, for example, in the Magna Carta), is superseded by English judgements of 'justice'. He later asserts primacy for the English in 'moral judgment' that cannot be let go of despite the fact that it is something 'the world does not require of us'; he asserts that 'a world of closed and closing societies desperately needs its prigs' (p. 162). Seemingly self-deprecatory, Fowles's self-identification as a 'prig' is nonetheless a claim for superiority. Being a prig is merely to be superior in a way that will not necessarily be recognized by others (testifying to their inferior perception). It is a superiority that neces-sitates a level of order and control over others, the others who are thereby allowed to live life free enough of burden and worries, it seems, to be able to childishly point to others' priggishness.

The stiff upper lip is a stereotype that is so common it has become a parody. Jolyon Forsyte in *The Man of Property,* volume one of the Forsyte Saga, is described as representing 'all that unconscious soundness, balance and vitality of fibre that made him and so many others of his class the core of the nation'.[15] It is an 'essential indi-vidualism', manifested in 'fibre' that is born 'from the natural isola-tion of his country's life'. The author presents the sense of self-possession through the specifics of soundness and balance, reverting through metaphor to a notion of the temperate self in which the humours are in balance, being the result of self-control ('the vitality of fibre') that keeps the self's passions and tempers in check. As such, Jolyon Forsyte can be traced back to Spenser's knight of Temperance, Sir Guyon.

Fowles outlines the English suspicion of emotions:

> The 'Wykehamist' (to be found in every class) exhibits a very typical sort of sheepish petulance when forced into the emotional declarations that would seem quite normal to any other race; he idolizes (not simply worships) common sense and non-interference; he will always see a good side in bad things ('*If people want to take drugs, why shouldn't' they?*'); and any emotional statement of opinion, however unjust, will immediately arouse his intense suspicion and probable hostility. (p. 159)

Fowles's recourse to the 'Wykehamist' is, of course, a highly class-based example, literally a former pupil of Winchester College, but one he claims 'found in every class'. The Wykehamist school motto is *Manners makyth man*, an emphasis upon bodily action that is at once conservative and, in the light of Butlerian theories of performativity in which acts constitute the self's reality, is telling of the relation between action and identity.[16] As we saw in Althusser's theories, it is precisely educational establishments such as Winchester College that drill mannerisms, bodily behaviour, into individuals – how to stand, sit, how to speak, what to wear – in order to create what Althusser sees as the regulated individual. The Wykehamist motto, one presumes, is not meant only to suggest the process of identity construction (although an important point of such education is to create a certain type of man) but that a good man is identifiable by the good manners that he 'instinctually' acts out, in much the same manner that Addison outlines in the early eighteenth century. The Wykehamist motto reveals, then, that emotional reticence is identified by external markers. The foundation to identity is aesthetic. When Fowles claims Wykehamists are to found in every class, he is witnessing the movement of the mannerisms of the upper class becoming the aspirational norm for all of society: everyone aspires to the markers of the higher classes but imitation is rarely fully successful because it depends on a sophisticated level of reading (of manners) that only those schooled in its lexicon can master.

Priestley links English self-control with the love of privacy: 'nearly everything in England that is of any importance is private and personal, that even our jokes have walls and hedges around them' (*English Humour*, p. 4). Gardens and personal reticence are cognate in their establishment of boundaries against others. For Santayana, geographical wanderings do not undermine the Englishman's self-control: 'he seldom allows his wanderings and discoveries to unhinge his home loyalties or ruffle his self-possession' (*Soliloquies*, p. 35). Like Fowles, Santayana links self-control to moral primacy. He asserts that 'The secret of English mastery is self-mastery. The Englishman establishes a sort of satisfaction and equilibrium in his inner man, and from that citadel of rightness he easily measures the value of everything that comes within his moral horizon' (p. 35). He continues: 'These self-sufficing Englishmen, in their reserve and decision, seemed to me truly men, creatures of fixed rational habit, people in whose somewhat inarticulate society one might feel safe and at home' (p. 5). English simplicity plays itself out, then, in the 'reserve' and 'decision' of the self-regulated man.

Self-control and rationality do not discount emotional profundity for Priestley. Instead, reservation is interpreted as a protectionist move that demonstrates a respect for and reverence of feeling. Despite such reservation, he qualifies, the English

> float through life on a deep if narrow stream of feeling; they commonly live in a matriarchy of the heart, unlike some of the more effusive races, who flaunt that heart as if it were some new mistress and use the emotions to decorate with some purely rational scheme of life; they live in such a deep intimacy with their feelings that they find it difficult and distasteful to reveal them; they have a horror of pretended feeling or easy emotion just because feeling to them is the key to the inner citadel, and to lose control of themselves is to reveal the last secret.
>
> (*English Humour*, pp. 18–19)

That this control is essentially masculine is revealed in Priestley's judgement of Fielding as a 'masculine writer: a man with a large cool mind' (p. 119). Characteristics of reserve merely indicate extent of control not paucity of emotion.

Although few English people would consider themselves as the 'new Israel' there is nonetheless a residual sense that the English in their exemplary self-control are, somehow, a chosen people. Orwell's assertion, cited above, that the English, God and Nature would be outraged 'to be ruled by foreigners' (*English People*, p. 13) expresses a deep-seated sense of pre-eminence. His is ultimately an argument for English superiority:

> They must have a clear notion of their own destiny and not listen either to those who tell them that England is finished or to those who tell them that the England of the past can return. [. . .] The world is sick of chaos and it is sick of dictatorship. Of all peoples the English are likeliest to find a way of avoiding both. (p. 48)

Orwell's suggestions for the English are tautological: they must, he is saying, be more English, which amounts to a deeply rooted sense of English superiority. They are, in a sense, their own judge and measure because there is none greater. Simplicity, among other things, will bring redemption from degradation: 'They must breed faster, work harder, and probably live more simply, think more deeply, get rid of their snobbishness' (p. 48). Although socialist in tone, Orwell's nationalism expresses the sense of the chosen people that Smith posits at the heart of nationalism,[17] and which nationalism owes to Protestantism:

> England can only fulfil its special mission if the ordinary English in the street can somehow get their hands on power. [. . .] By the end of another decade it will be finally clear whether England is to survive as a great nation or not. And if the answer is to be 'Yes', it is the common people who must make it so. (p. 48)

The mutually constructive qualities of land and character mean that in mythologies of Englishness, the English are as simple as their 'green and pleasant' land. The mythology of simplicity persists in influential writing as it communicates the transparency of a country-side that reveals truth to its redeemed readers, and renders the English a simple, yet discerning, self-controlled elect. It is far from being the innocent characteristic that Scruton, for one, turns to for stability. As the next chapter shows, simplicity implicates those who do not adequately express or appreciate it. Simplicity and straightforward-ness are far from benign. It can no longer be asserted, as Colls does in his 2002 book, invoking Orwell's claims for the English: 'the English of today are still the same people who will hold open a door, say "please", "cheers", and "thank you", and do not vote for extremist political parties' (p. 2).

CHAPTER FOUR

THE PROTESTANT AESTHETIC AND ISLAMOPHOBIA

As an essentially oppositional aesthetic, simplicity produces dispositions that eschew the ornamented, and because of expectations of transparency (that bestow on the observer rationality and self-control), they reject the non-simple in moral and ethical terms: ostentatious people who are oblivious to the beauty of simplicity are undiscriminating. Unable to discern, they lack rationality and the perspective needed to control unruly passions and impulses. As Scruton implies, those who do not understand the beauty of the simple are ridiculous, but also potentially dangerous in their circulation of spurious ideas. This chapter considers Islamophobia as a phenomenon that is the outworking of English simplicity's oppositional impulse. I use the term Islamophobia quite self-consciously as a term that foregrounds the non-rational as the discussion is focused on the siting of anti-Islamic prejudice, the phobia, within an unconscious aesthetic register. Its commonly cited definition from the report by the Runnymede Trust Commission on British Muslims and Islamophobia, *Islamophobia: A Challenge for us All*, is: 'a shorthand way of referring to dread or hatred of Islam – and, therefore, to fear or dislike of all or most Muslims', which highlights viscerality – dread and hatred – although the substantial analysis of the report is focused on rationalized prejudice.[1] This chapter considers a range of Islamophobic articulations to consider how the aesthetics and dispositions of Englishness – based on the aesthetic of simplicity outlined in the previous three chapters – informs the specific construction of rejected Muslim identities. I look at a sample of anti-Islamic sentiment in interviews, newspapers and Martin Amis's collection of writings on 9/11, *The Second Plane*, that all show how Islam is constructed as an externalized and elaborate religion in opposition to English simplicity's guarantee of interiorization, honesty, rationality and control. Islamophobia is shown to be motivated by aesthetic, rather than rational, concerns. Although sometimes couched in the language of rational and reasonable discussion, anti-Islamic sentiment is often the expression of a more visceral response to Muslims that taps into a set of seemingly wide-ranging stereotypes.

The 1997 Runnymede Trust's *Islamophobia: A Challenge for us All*, begins with the discussion of a British naval officer's rhetorical question: 'Where would you pray to Mecca on a submarine?' (p. 1).[2] The comment, although recognized as 'presumably some sort of joke', is considered representative and the report goes on to combat, in general terms, the officer's evident ignorance of Muslim prayer and, in more empirical terms, specific ignorance of the British merchant navy's dependence on so-called 'lascars', Muslim seamen, during the Second World War. The report concludes its short discussion by speculating that 'What the officer presumably had in mind, alas, was a notion that it is inappropriate for British Muslims to play a part in defending their country since Britain is not really, he believes, their country. They therefore cannot be expected, he believes further, to be loyal to it.' The report identifies a possible set of negative beliefs behind the officer's comment, yet the statement is more telling of the officer's assumptions and attitude than the report reveals.

Its very rhetoricity, 'Where would you pray to Mecca on a submarine?', suggests an expectation on the part of the speaker that his is 'common sense'; jokes, after all, only work through the expectation of shared cultural assumptions. As such it works against an unarticulated sense of normality: a sense of normal submariner behaviour and of normal prayer. The naval officer's comment about Islamic practice measures the aberration of explicit Muslim practices – perceived as unduly elaborate – against an (unarticulated) norm of English habitual practices or *habitus*. It is English *habitus*, not rational argument, that plays an essential role in shaping the ways in which the English and British perceive Muslims. This normality is articulated in two key ways. First, in citing Mecca, the officer is constructing the Muslim as submitting to a *place* and not a deity: the Muslim is associated with Mecca, the 'normal' Christian implicitly with a non-situated God. Second, the 'Where' of the question suggests the impossibility of incorporating Muslim activities (and therefore Muslim bodies) in a submarine. The 'normal' Christian prayer, the 'where' implies, does not need a 'where' – it is assimilatable into everyday submariner life and is likely to be deemed internalized enough not to disrupt activities. Muslims are not only rendered 'foreign' through association with another country, but rendered physically unassimilatable. Muslim prayer is doubly situated, then, both in an alien place (Mecca) and in an unincorporatable practice (prayer): it is not only ideologically situated elsewhere but materially obstructive: it physically cannot exist within the body of the submarine, and by extension, the navy and the body politic, Britain. Such prayer, the logic goes, will be disruptive to patriotism and submariner activity. Hence, the report identifies the unspoken assumption that Muslim prayer will take precedence over the necessary security function of the navy.

What this rhetorical question – 'Where would you pray to Mecca on a submarine?' – reveals are some of the specific, not generalized, prejudices of Islamophobia. Focused here on bodies and practices, these prejudices' very materiality constructs Islam as an externalized religion. Its externality means that behaviour is not conceived as separable from the individual, which is often the case of the nominal Church of England adherent, for example, whose prayer uttered in a moment of crisis can be seen as at odds with who they profess to be; as Santayana notes, the Christian is envisioned as someone who can *be* and *do* entirely different things (see p. 89). Muslims *are* their habitual practices of prayer: the disruptive prayer works metonymically to represent the (disruptive) individual.

The troubling body and practice of the Muslim are interpreted as a physical imposition that, materially constituted, rejects secular, liberal values. If secular society values the neutrality of public space, then, as Elizabeth Poole has concluded, the liberal secular agenda (that she identifies with *The Guardian*), 'marginalizes religion to the private realm' – forging an equation of progressive religion with privacy – and as such 'render[s] "Islamic" practices irrational and barbaric"'.[3] This equation – that the public nature of Islamic religious practice makes it unfit for the modern secular nation-state – does not account for the sense in which Islam is presented frequently as an *unavoidably* public religious identity: those who condemn its public nature simultaneously speak about Islam as a set of practices that cannot be relegated to a private space. The apparent impossibility of Muslim prayer onboard a submarine exposes the way in which Islam's spiritual practices, such as prayer, are represented as unavoidably and disruptively public, encroaching on others' personal – and by extension, political – space. As a public, externalized religion, made up (it seems overwhelmingly) of visible practices, Islam becomes a religion that is registered on an aesthetic level rather than a rational, discursive one. The result is that Muslims are not just sometimes treated as texts to be read, but they are conceived of as surfaces, as pure practice, not rational beings to be engaged with. The perceived materiality of Islam is gestured towards in recent scholarship that notes the way in which prejudice against Muslims focuses on physical markers and is thereby cognate with race prejudice. Pnina Werbner notes that violence against Asians is, in fact, against 'the discrete national and religious icons of subgroupings within the broader Asian collectivity'.[4] That prejudice is based on visual response is also suggested by Nasar Meer and Tariq Modood with their reflection that 'the majority of Muslims who report experiencing street-level discrimination recount – as testimonies to the Runnymedes' 2004 follow-up Commission bear witness – that they do so when they appear "conspicuously Muslim" more than when they do not'.[5]

In tracing contemporary Englishness to its past in Reformation English doctrines, this book is not narrating a history of anti-Islamic sentiment. Instead, the focus is on aspects of contemporary Islamophobia that are a by-product of a specifically oppositional Englishness that can easily masquerade as a benign Englishness of simplicity, honesty and self-possession. This means that rather than an articulated – and therefore disputable – argument against Islam, opposition is situated in the English aesthetic of simplicity, a simplicity that communicates a supra-rationalism, morality and self-control that renders Islam (among other things) as necessarily irrational, immoral and uncontrolled. Unlike explicit articulations of anti-Islamic sentiment, English aesthetics continue without recourse to argument and are not open to refutation. The distinction is important because a trajectory of inherited Islamophobia leads to an assumption that combating prejudice will expel anti-Islamic ideas and sentiments. Instead, because it is a specific construction of Englishness (that itself engenders Islamophobia) that has been passed on, the expulsion of Islamophobic sentiments is dependent upon an interrogation of Englishness. The problem is revealed to be more fundamental and based on the interrelation of Englishness (based in an aesthetic of simplicity and self-possession) and Islamophobia (based on the expulsion of the ostentatious and elaborate, irrational and the uncontrolled). The point is one of attention. Jean-Paul Sartre expresses in 1948 in his treatise on Anti-Semitism: 'The more one is absorbed in fighting Evil, the less one is tempted to place the Good in question'.[6] If the focus is on what is delineated as evil (Islamism), then the 'good' (Englishness) is left unarticulated and never interrogated.

There is, of course, a history of English anti-Islamic sentiment.[7] Although there are clear instances of opposition to 'Turks' in the early modern and intervening period, what this book argues is that it is the specific Reformed constructions of Englishness (necessarily always with its perceived enemies – Jews, the French, Turks, but mostly Catholics – in mind) that have been passed on and that play an important role in contemporary Islamophobia. This oppositional character of Englishness is apparent in Edmund Spenser's *The Faerie Queene*'s Redcrosse Knight who slays not only fantastical Catholic monsters (such as Error) but also the three Saracens, Sans Foi, Sans Joy and Sans Loi (Islam here depicted allegorically as being without faith, without joy and without law). David J. Vitkus argues that Spenser is no doubt borrowing from medieval narratives in which Christian knights fight Saracen enemies.[8] Turks were placed within a Christian teleology in which they acted as the 'scourge of God'[9], a term used by Marlowe's Tamburlaine to describe himself as he dies (II. v. iii).[10] Historically, the relation between the English and Turks was ambivalent at best. Protestants welcomed Ottoman oppression of Catholic states and the Ottoman threat forced Charles V to concede freedom of religious practices to Lutheran sectarians in the 1520s and 30s (p. 212). Elizabeth, through Walsingham, even sought military alliance with the Ottoman sultanate, but Walsingham hoped that antagonism between Spain and Turkey, who he called the two 'limbs of the Devil' might lead to 'the suppression of them both' (fn. 30). Luther's attitude is one in which Protestantism sees threat in the Turk. He writes in his *Table Talk*: 'The spirit of Antichrist is the Pope, his flesh the Turk. One attacks the Church physically, the other spiritually' (fn.19).

The similarity between early modern prejudice against Turks and present-day expressions of Islamophobia are due, then, to their function as oppositional to Protestantism.[11] Viktus's description of medieval and early modern sentiment is strongly suggestive of modern prejudices: 'The Muslim rulers were then represented as tyrants who exercise an absolute and arbitrary power, especially over life and death. They are irrational and unjust, fond of beheading and other cruel forms of punishments and torture' (p. 200). The characteristics delineated here are more telling of how Protestant Christians saw themselves at this time: the evil enemy is the mirror image of the pious self. The tyrant, irrational and unjust, reflected back a Protestantism that purported true freedom, true rationality and true justice. This is evident in the tenacity of prejudice against non-Protestants in early modern writings. While Catholics were abject because of their excessive ornamentation, Islam in its rejection of imagery could be placed at another extreme, the secretly Catholic Babington is reported to have condemned the 'Turkish' rejection of naturalistic art as 'too superstitious'.[12] Vitkus's reading of book V of the *The Faerie Queene* is instructive. Spenser's Arthur here fights the Islamic 'Souldan', a figure of military cruelty, of 'lawlesse power and tortious wrong', identified as a figure of Philip II of Spain. The Souldan is destroyed by his own horses, who were 'halfe ded' (V. viii. 28), 'an image of oppressed subjects rebelling against and destroying an unjust overlord' Vitkus explains (p. 220). The allegory conflates Popish and Turkish tyranny and injustice, constructing the Protestant cause as 'honour' and 'right' (V. viii. 30).

English opposition to Catholics and Turks is markedly visual. They were both understood to be guilty because of their sensual luxury. Duessa, the whore of Babylon, wears a 'Persian mitre on her hed' (I. i. 13) and is accompanied by Sans Foy (without faith). Sans Foy misreads the cross ('Curse upon that Crosse . . . that keepes thy body from bitter fit', I. ii. 18), which he can only conceive of in superstitious terms, as Vitkus comments, like 'an amulet worn to avert evil' (p. 222). Although the link between Duessa and Rome is recognized in critical readings, her link to Islam is often overlooked – Vitkus underscores Babylon's relation to Cairo and Baghdad, citing the Geneva Bible that states that the Fall of Babylon will be accompanied by the fall of 'all strange religions, as of the Jews, Turks and others'.[13] Kermode has noted the oppositional character of Spenser's aesthetics, in which Duessa and Sansfoy (II. xiii), are adorned with Persian mitre, and bells and flounces of 'wanton palfry', which 'signify the union of popish flummery and oriental presumption', qualities that oppose English plain style.[14] Depictions of Muslims in Spenser is, then, inextricably caught up in Protestant self-identification on a specifically aesthetic register.

As shown in the previous chapters, the transposition of Protestant theology into an aesthetic and thereby into English *habitus* means that Englishness subsists of a mythology that is antagonistic to the aesthetics and practices of certain religions in a way that is completely separate from any conscious adherence to a faith. The tastes and qualities of Englishness function, after all, as an invisible norm, an unreflected pre-judgement, as seen in the naval officer's comment: it is essentially non-rational, unchosen and perpetuated without conscious or rational engagement. Rarely articulated, it is difficult to identify, never mind scrutinize. What is essential to note is that the naval officer is not objecting on any doctrinal grounds to Islamic prayer: it is the aesthetics and activities of prayer that are instinctively felt to be abnormal and dangerous. It is not a religious sentiment, but an aesthetic and practical one that is the corpse of a distant and specific formulation of Protestantism and its related aesthetic, simplicity. That there is no belief system engaged with suggests it does not represent a clash of religious beliefs; recent scholarship indicates that, perhaps because of overlapping agendas, religious groups are on the whole less likely to express prejudice.[15]

Anti-Muslim sentiment is often identified in vague terms, and most often as a cognitive practice. It is, for example, seen as 'endemic to the European mindset', as Allen expresses it.[16] Fatoviç identifies an oppositional logic – founded in the anti-Catholicism of the English Reformation that is 'a thoroughly political and historically contingent activity that revolves around oppositions whose origins are often forgotten' – but locates it in the rational sphere, analogous to Allen's 'mindset'.[17] The Runnymede report, cited at the opening of this chapter, also conceptualizes 'unfounded hostility to Muslims' (as they define Islamophobia) as mindsets, conceptual practices, ignoring the force of aesthetics or non-cognitive attitudes. This study is therefore unusual in focusing precisely on those aspects of discrimination that function beyond rational engagement. While Martin Reisigl and Ruth Wodak critique Albert Memmi's term heterophobia because it neglects the 'active and aggressive part of discrimination', analyses of Islamophobia tend to focus exclusively on precisely its cognitive, conscious aspects.[18] Yet, the opposition apparent in the naval officer's comment is visceral rather than conceptual. Opposition to Islam as an exterior, rather than rational, activity suggests that attention also needs to be focused on externals, and to the symbiotic relationship of aesthetic elements to visceral dispositions. The reciprocal functioning of disposition (what one likes) and an aesthetic (the thing liked is reified), constructs an 'Englishness' that is situated in the individual but also necessarily in places and things. Dispositions of openness,

rationality and self-control may be interior qualities but in their relation to Englishness they are intimately related to an externalized aesthetic of simplicity. As an essentially oppositional construction (the
'not truly' English will not like or value the same things) means that
English dispositions and aesthetics are meant to distinguish homely
from alien practice. Attention to the aesthetic sphere is admittedly
also not new: Edward Said for one noted Lord Cromer's rejection of
'Oriental' disorderliness that he related to their 'picturesque streets',
but based his analysis on a Foucauldian power-knowledge relationship in which aesthetics are an expression or representation of a
consciously held rejection of foreign values.[19] The logic of the dispos-
ition-aesthetic symbiosis is that valued aesthetics are rendered natural, so that aesthetic judgements are considered equivalent to moral
ones. The negative judgements about Muslim aesthetics as unnat-
ural, according to this logic, can only lead to the alienation of Muslims and restrict their participation in the cultural, political and civic
life of Britain.

National character is often taken at face value, and because of the
benign nature of much of English mythology – simplicity, rationality, justice – it is left uninterrogated, as demonstrated in an article on
'The British Veil Wars' by Sevgi Kiliç. The article deftly outlines two
British court cases in detail (both English, one in Manchester, one in
London) and helpfully makes a distinction between political and cultural structures and their effect on Muslim experience in Britain.
'Despite the "assimilationist turn" of British multiculturalism and
the popular reaction against the *niqab* in the public domain', she
writes, 'it is the political structures and political opportunities that
have been decisive in shaping the non-regulation of the *hijab*, *jilbab*
and the *niqab* in Britain'.[20] In the body of the article, then, negative
cultural attitudes are set against the positive workings of justice in
the courts. Yet she concludes her article with recourse to national
identity, albeit British national identity (but which is recognizably
English myth) that is celebrated and implicitly located as foundational to the practice of court justice. She points to the political
mechanisms that 'serve against the arbitrary banning of *jilbabs* and
niqabs and are the threshold of what James Fishkin (1992) calls "pro-
cedural fairness" or in everyday parlance – British pragmatism'
(p. 451). To extend Kiliç's metaphor of the threshold, she portrays
British (or rather English) pragmatism as a secure interior space, and
its political activities work at its threshold. 'British pragmatism' as

metaphorical home is undermined by her assertion that Muslim experience within the real home (the cultural sphere outside the courts) is hostile: assimilation is demanded and the *niqab* rejected. From the fair practices of the law courts, Kiliç presumes a cultural foundation of 'British pragmatism' that does not add up to the cultural norms that she traces in wider society.

English mythology appears benign: the characteristics of simplicity, rationality, self-control and liberality are indeed not inherently problematic qualities; but the specific significance of English aesthetic simplicity (that itself signifies transparency, rationality, self-control and liberality) is oppositional – continuing anti-Catholic and Protestant partisanship and positing itself not against complexity, but against the elaborate and the ornate and claiming a unique access to knowledge. Paul Bagguley and Yasmin Hussain's research considers the preference for the St. George flag over the Union Jack as a marker of national affiliation among British Pakistani Muslims, demonstrating the degree to which the group do not perceive Englishness as oppositional. Whereas the Union Jack is seen as 'the property of the far right and a symbol of the beliefs of the BNP', the English flag is seen as 'more expressive of an "authentic" national identity that has not been soiled by racism'.[21] A 30-year-old explains that taxi drivers and teenagers display the St. George's flag because 'They are trying to show that England means something to them and that England is our team. We are from England'. The affiliation is not dependent, he asserts, on specific cultural markers: 'if you say they are only English if they sit down and have roast beef and potatoes then it is not going to happen' (p. 215). The cultural markers of authentic Englishness are not deemed alienating, like the British Union Jack, but like roast beef and potatoes appear benign, and the English flag even innocent enough to be appropriated by the Muslim community.

Whereas the majority of anti-Islamic sentiment is what I will call unreflective Islamophobia (found in writings, newspapers and websites, whose authors or primary audience are 'ordinary' people and who articulate instinctual attitudes that are not reflected upon), there is a significant articulation of what I will call rationalized Islamophobia. The latter is represented here by broadsheet articles on Muslims and by Martin Amis's collection of essays and short stories, *The Second Plane*. Rationalized Islamophobia is characterized by recourse to reason: Islamophobia defended as a reasonable activity, if not *the* supremely rational activity. It has become possible to defend Islamophobic comments through arguing that discussion about religion is not only possible, but necessary, in a rational society, as seen in Polly Toynbee's assertion: 'I am an Islamophobe [. . .] Religiophobia is highly rational'.[22] But as the naval officer's comment reveals, the articulation of Islamophobia is rarely so rational (and even impossibly rational in the sense that rational defence of a phobia is scarcely logical). Such recourse to rationalism reflects the priority of rational debate in society but is possibly more sinisterly reflective of an elision of any non-rational elements of behaviour.

Amis's collection, *The Second Plane*, is pertinent to this study because it represents both rationalized Islamophobia and reflects in depth about visceral aspects of belief (although not his own prejudices but those of the Islamists he writes about). Conflating literary and religious practices, he suggests that the 'inherited and unexamined formulations' of literature (for Amis distinct from the novelty of Joyce's *Ulysees*) can be repeated in human activity.[23] What is formulaic in literature is analogous to the bigotry within society: 'After all, prejudices are cliché's, they are secondhand hatreds.'[24] Key to both activities – cliché and prejudice – is the act of borrowing that Amis repeatedly vilifies in his collection. Religion more generally is included in his critique of cliché and prejudice: it too is derivative. He writes of going to chapel and his rejection of it:

> What you got, so it seemed, was a community and a language. My apostacy, at the age of nine, was vehement. Clearly, I didn't want the shared words, the shared identity. I forswore chapel. (*The Second Plane*, pp. 14–15)

According to Amis, chapel submerged him into the secondhand, into an indistinguishable, homogeneous mass, and he bolts in the name of individuality and freedom. Borrowing is lazy and leads to bad attitudes: only rationality, and its consort creativity, can save the individual who is seemingly bombarded by the prejudices of his environment.

And yet Amis's *The Second Plane* is overrun with cliché, what Arthur Bradley and Andrew Tate have labelled his 'war for cliché' (*The New Atheist Novel*, ch. 2). It is apparent that Amis's own writings on Islam, despite their poetic creativity at times, demonstrate inherited (and in his terms, unoriginal) dispositions and attitudes. In

Amis's defence, this may be partly due to the codification of Islamic – and 'Western'– qualities that he talks about that are themselves so formulaic that it has become difficult to find a vocabulary to talk about Muslims without recourse to stereotype. As Bradley and Tate, indeed, insist: 'the post-9/11 world poses an imaginative challenge that [Amis's] fiction has not (at least not yet) risen to meet' (p. 53). But more fundamentally, Amis's concurrent rejection of cliché, prejudice and religion as secondhand, and his own derivative writing undermines his polarizing of cliché and individuality. In the above account of his rejection of religion, his forswearing of chapel is suggestive of the paradox at the heart of his writing. His repeated use of the term 'shared' here – 'shared words', 'shared identity' – works with his description of the chapel as 'a community and a language' to identify the chapel as primarily social. The terms 'community', 'language', and 'shared' define human society generally, leading to the suspicion that Amis's rejection of religion and its 'shared words' and 'shared identity' is a doomed attempt to escape the necessarily 'shared' nature of social human existence.

Amis not only ignores the force of inherited dispositions on individuals – what Bourdieu identifies as *habitus* – but disregards the bricolage nature of all creative effort – that even the creative writer is born into a culture's specific construction and categorization of the world, and that even new or individual articulations are always both iterative and innovative. There is a complex relation between identity that is received (one's language and culture are not of one's own choosing) and those aspects of identity that are chosen (within overlapping, contradictory or multiple identities, self-positioning or self-fashioning is inevitable). As Bikhu Parekh has written, community identities are simultaneously open to change and limited by historical structures. National identities are made up of 'a cluster of interrelated and relatively open-ended tendencies and impulses pulling in different directions and capable of being developed and balanced in different ways', but also:

> Its historically evolved structures persist over time and restrict choices. To say that each generation is free to redefine its national identity in the light of its needs is to ignore the basic fact that its very definition of the needs and of what it considers acceptable ways of satisfying them are shaped by the inherited way of life.[25]

With every repetition, there is the slippage, the necessity of difference but also the necessity of continuity; as Derrida has argued, within repetition there is always both identity and alterity: the logic of iterability 'ties repetition to alterity'.[26]

Simultaneous with Amis's cliché (despite his war against it), is his passing on of 'inherited and unexamined formulations' and not only at the level of articulation but at the level of disposition. Although Amis claims he is not an Islamophobe because 'a phobia is an irrational fear, and it is not irrational to fear something that says it wants to kill you' (*Second Plane*, p. x), he expresses dispositions that function at a visceral or habitual, not rational, level. His statement here testifies to the specific nature of his negotiation of Islam in the light of Islamic fundamentalist terrorist threat: he approaches Muslims as surface, not rational people. He is responding to the 'something' that 'says' it threatens. In light of the title of his book, *The Second Plane*, it seems to be the iconic that Amis is reading. It is Islamic *things* (the plane perhaps) that he is responding to, but also the Muslim, not as rational being, but as (some) *thing*, as text.

Bradley and Tate have already demonstrated the way in which, despite his equation of unthinking borrowing with cliché, Amis posits aesthetics as working at a non-rational level. Despite his assertion that 'A novel is a rational undertaking; it is reason at play, perhaps, but it is still reason', he also describes imaginative writings as 'mysterious', working 'beneath the threshold of consciousness, and without the intercession of reason' (p. 12). The intimation here is perhaps a Romantic one of genius mysteriously generating sublime works of art, but it is still not rational. What concerns this study is the extent to which Amis demonstrates some degree of perception regarding the non-rational elements in an individual's articulations (whether literary writing or attitudes) and yet categorically insists upon rationality as the key criteria for (both stylistically and morally) 'good' writing. Rather than allowing his identification of the non-rational to critique and modify the rationalist agenda, he instead sets no limits to the realm of rationality's sway: in his war against cliché, even in imaginative writing, reason is all.

Amis is also a useful focus for this study because far from being a 'secular Scripture', for him literature is *the* secular art (p. 16). Literature for Amis, as Bradley and Tate outline, is 'individuality, originality and freedom of expression' (p. 39). His claim that 'Writing *is* freedom' (*The Second Plane*, p. 51) invokes his adversity to the opposite qualities he identified in cliché, prejudice and the chapel. Again, the distinction is hard to maintain as his own writing demonstrates in his passing on of secondhand tropes. He reifies literature in a way that distances it from any religious ties with a fervour that questions his stark dissolution of the religious and secular and, as such, his disavowal of a religion whose qualities so echo his own secular mantra.[27]

This chapter will now consider the ways in which Islamophobia functions as a set of dispositions (despite disclaimers by writers like Amis), shaped by the norms of mythologies of Englishness and their related aesthetics of simplicity. After a discussion of the generally visceral nature of Islamophobia, I will go on to consider the representation of Muslims in the light of mythologies of Englishness centred on simplicity, echoing the qualities outlined in the previous chapter. Although a larger set of characteristics are identifiable (the Runnymede report identifies 'closed' views of Islam as 'monolithic', 'separate', 'inferior', 'enemy' and 'manipulative', p. 5), I am focusing solely on those qualities that are antithetical to English simplicity: the Muslim as ostentatious (in distinction to the reserved English); as dishonest (as opposed to the open-souled); as urban (opposed to rural); as marked by rituals that are complex (as opposed to straightforward) and empty (as opposed to meaningful); irrational (opposed to rational); uncontrolled (versus English self-possession); and tyrannical (opposed to an Englishness of free choice).

* * *

Elizabeth Poole's study of the representation of Muslims in the British media, published in 2002, notes the 'strong consensual interpretive frameworks that exist with regard to Muslims in mainstream British society' (p. 247). The consensus is often identified as 'cultural-racism' rather than 'straightforward colour racism'.[28] Opinion polls carried out on British attitudes to Muslims demonstrate to some degree the extent to which the British perceive Muslim values as incompatible with their own. The results of opinion polls, outlined in Clive Field's article 'Islamophobia in Contemporary Britain', demonstrate a snapshot of changing attitudes towards Muslims in Britain. The evidence may be problematic as data – often a tick-box affair of agreement with pre-set statements, and largely commissioned by the media in the light of national events – and as such, they do not represent a nuanced picture of attitudes. However, they demonstrate a sizeable and distinct perception that British and Muslim values are at odds. Polls demonstrate a perceived disjunction on the behalf of white British citizens between Muslim and normative British values, with nearly half of one poll claiming that 'the country would begin to lose its identity if more Muslims came'.[29] Muslims are seen as choosing and preferring insularity and Islam is increasingly seen as a threat to Western liberal democracy.[30]

Even where anti-Islamic sentiment is rationalized or explained, it nonetheless functions on a visceral-aesthetic level. Couched in reasonable terms, much of the 'veil debate' following Jack Straw's column in the *Lancashire Telegraph* in 2006 treats female, veiled Muslims not as rational individuals, but as a text to be interpreted (although Straw himself is more careful in his writings). Commentators become exegetes who can reveal the 'true' motivations behind the sign of the veil, the individuals' intentions negated. In her article, 'Multiculturalism hasn't worked: Let's rediscover Britishness', 8 October 2006, Patience Wheatcroft in *The Daily Telegraph* demonstrates a visceral response to the aesthetics of Islam that is couched in ostensibly rational terms.[31] The article is useful in terms of explicitly setting up Islam against an Englishness defined by a latent Protestantism, although one that subscribes to a Protestant ethic not a Protestant aesthetic. Like Amis, she asserts a rationalist and straight-talking agenda while her writing is strongly rhetorical and shaped by only half-articulated attitudes. Muslims are ultimately defined as deceptive (hampering free speech), as aggressively public (through their clothing) and ultimately as unduly ostentatious when measured against a mythological reserved and simple Englishness.

Wheatcroft welcomes Straw's sparking of a debate as a move against the 'tyranny of political correctness', framing her piece as a contribution to a newly rational discussion that nonetheless undermines the principles of 'straight talking' with a choice of vocabulary that is rhetorically complex: the term 'tyranny' works on an implicit level to conflate political correctness with oppressive regimes and is sufficiently vague to allow manipulation of any facts she engages with. Her description of political correctness as a 'doctrine' that 'dictated' (albeit 'that all beliefs should be allowed to flourish') creates a discourse that implicitly underlines political correctness as a quasi-religious practice aligned with stereotypes of the Islamic practices she goes on to discuss, at odds with the English freedoms she is defending. Her article is representative of the 'assimilationist turn' in attitudes to minority communities, as she paints the picture of the long history of Britain as a 'happily integrated society' in which immigrants have 'been welcomed and assimilated'. The grammatical ambiguity of this statement (have immigrants been passive to their assimilation or does welcome lead them to choose to assimilate?) suggests both that the host community needs to be active in encouraging assimilation but that they don't hold full responsibility: like being welcomed, assimilation is something the host is partly responsible for, although it is also something that, on the surface at least, is chosen by properly grateful migrants.

Wheatcroft's argument for the Church of England as 'the predominant faith in the country' and that 'cohesion' depends upon 'a degree of confidence in core British ideas', conflates Christianity and Britishness, the former providing the latter with a moral foundation. While deriding John Major's 'hovis-style vision of bicycling delivery boys doffing their caps to village worthies' (although it was old maids cycling to communion), she asserts 'tolerance, politeness and compassion' as British core values, indeed as 'Christian values' that 'prevail' despite the decline in the 'church-going habit'. It becomes clear that British values are based in a set of moral values that are attached to a specific religion (Christianity) that is nonetheless relegated to a past heritage, a habit now given up. So while arguing for the predominance of the Church of England, she elides spiritual activity or actual religious belief, and instead asserts its relevance only as a moral influence. The foundational identity she is defending is already shrouded in a mythological mist. Although explicitly speaking of Britain, her descriptors and emphasis in the Church of England clearly indicate a mythological Englishness.

Her discussion of the veil is framed by her metaphorical use of the term in her second paragraph, where she punningly commends Straw for having 'raised the veil on an issue that, privately, many will have admitted to finding disturbing'. The 'many' here are reticent and private individuals, underlining the polarization of the privacy of (correct) British opinion versus the public nature of Muslim's clothing statements. The veil as metaphor signifies wrongful hiding and covering, and its removal is an act of illumination, openness and honesty. Even before Wheatcroft writes explicitly about Muslim veils, four paragraphs later, the veil is already a suspicious article of deception and repression with English free speech as victim. With this frame, the reader is set up to assent to her loaded, undefended and vacuous statement that the 'full veil is something different' (to the normal spectrum of clothes choices). Wheatcroft taps into widespread assumptions of the deceptiveness of Muslims (a survey in 1990 revealed a majority of white British who were cautious, if not outright suspicious, about the trustworthiness of all Muslims).[32]

When explicitly engaging with the Islamic veil, Wheatcroft describes it as a 'barrier', arguing that it 'unites those who nestle behind such garments and makes it harder for them to integrate with the bulk of the population'. Her claim that the veil 'unites those' presents a solid group identified by a gender-neutral pronoun: wearing the veil is no longer something practised by individual women in different ways (the *burka*, *niqab* or *hijab* covers different parts of the body, head and face) and for different reasons (following different cultural traditions). The neutrality of the pronoun 'those' allows the possibility that Wheatcroft's comments extend to Muslims as a whole and even invokes, implicitly, the male extremists who carried out the 9/11 and 7/7 bombings. The image of 'nestle behind' suggests a site of comfort and security that is logically denied those on the other side of the veil, who are instead constructed as exposed, the implication is, to danger. The term 'behind' underscores the spatial sense of a barrier between two spaces (us and them). The veil does not merely cover, it hides, separates and demarcates. It is not the expression of religious belief or a choice, it is not even a practice that provokes discussion, or even an item of clothing; instead it is a provocative 'statement' of 'separation', alienation and non-integration, not just of difference (Wheatcroft differentiates it from the normal variety in clothing in a 'society in which just about any style of dress is imaginable').

Because it is represented by Wheatcroft as a 'uniform that they choose to wear', the veil is constructed as part of a spectrum of individual rational choice that makes it suitable for public debate. Wheatcroft's respect for choice seems out of place in an article that is demanding assimilation and unequivocally criticizing the veil. Her statement: 'If a woman should wish to shroud herself in black from head to foot and cover her face all but for a slit for her to peer through, then it is her right to do so' reads differently from the rest of the elegant prose. The awkwardly long opening clause, in its almost mesmeric, pedestrian rhythm, seemingly ventriloquizes an equally tedious opinion. The phrase 'her right to do so' suggests political correctness as her target, attacked at the opening of the article. Wheatcroft communicates disapproval and even mockery at odds with the ostensible liberality of the statement. She ends the article with a plea to those Muslims who may wish 'to play a full role in British society', that they 'should realize that they are making that more difficult' because of 'the uniform they choose to wear'. By choosing to label the veil as 'uniform', veil-wearing Muslims become school children or an army. (Who describes their national or religious dress as 'uniform'?) Contained within the discourse of liberalism and choice, Wheatcroft constructs various illogical and unarticulated logics. Although she seeks to push the 'veil affair' into public debate and rational argument, she falls upon 'Christian values' in which Christianity is a convenient rally-cry rather than a set of beliefs, and Britishness is 'tolerance, politeness and compassion', a conveniently vague and incontestible set of qualities in which only politeness is a recognizable part of national English mythology.

The article functions, as the naval officer's question did, against a set of assumptions about 'normal' behaviour. Wheatcroft gestures towards the more rational discussions regarding veil-wearing: that veils mask the face, hindering communication. But in the light of the fact that not all veils cover the face and that attacks against Muslims are mostly against women wearing any kind of head covering and against all Muslims wearing religiously specific clothing, there seems to be a more general, and admittedly not clearly articulated, opposition to 'difference' and importantly, 'separateness'.[33] Wheatcroft's attitude is representative, it seems, of British opinion. Returning to the evidence of polls, one set of results revealed a minority who found veils frightening or intimidating while a majority agreed with Jack Straw that the veil is a 'practical [although, it seems, from the previous opinion, not a literal] barrier to good race relations and a mark of segregation' (Field, p. 460). Those who felt Muslims needed to make more effort to integrate rose from a significant minority to an overwhelming majority between 2004 and 2006 and in another poll coherent British Islamic identity was deemed a 'bad thing' by a majority.[34]

Wheatcroft's article is important because it demonstrates a recourse to a 'C of E' Englishness that identifies itself explicitly in undeniably positive terms (tolerance, politeness and compassion) and yet an oppositional impulse is discernible which draws on a set of assumptions about Muslim practice. The veil signifies deceit and its meaning is deciphered as one of 'separation' by the onlooker, it is unnecessarily ostentatious (a 'statement' and a 'uniform') and as such is an imposition into the public realm. The 'difference' of Muslim practices is asserted against an unarticulated value and so it is difficult to draw firm conclusions, but the statement makes sense if the norm is taken to correspond to the explicitly articulated sense of English simplicity that was explored in the previous three chapters. Wheatcroft's invocation of a 'C of E' set of traditions to oppose Muslim aesthetic practice is repeated in recent BNP and EDL arguments that have mobilized Islamophobia as central to their politic agenda.[35] Her argument, despite her morals of 'tolerance, politeness, and compassion' – are almost wholly aesthetic and she defends not beliefs but nativity plays and Christmas decorations. For the Navy officer and Wheatcroft, the habitual praying habits and clothing choices of Muslims only seem intricate and excessive against an apparently reasonable norm that corresponds to the dispositions of the Englishman (certainly not the devout or enthusiastic Christian) that privileges an English aesthetic of moderation and simplicity.

The assumption is that excessive practice demonstrates a basic misunderstanding of reasonable activity, and of a misreading of the world. While the English taste for simplicity marks their privileged discernment, so Muslim excessive ritual and aesthetic practice marks them as dislocated from reality and reason. Ritual activity (prayer or the veil) is represented as demanding the disengagement of the rational mind – just as Reformed spontaneity and rationality was constructed as more authentic than Catholic ritual. Such ritual is considered oppressive to its adherents and, because of its dampening of rational capacity, is only one step away from manipulated aggression. The Protestant eschewal of ritual and its self-representation as a pure, uncluttered religion, rationally chosen and intellectually engaging, is one that is undermined when one considers the ritualized nature of all human activity, its performative and constructive, not merely expressive, force. When Protestantism was at its most assertively radical in the early modern civil war years, it was nonetheless still ritualized and formulaic; the individual was subject to the forces of their religious context – the forging of new traditions – as tradition itself was subject to the force of individuals. The spiritual autobiography, or conversion narrative, contains as a necessary element the radical conversion of the individual. It was a genre that grew up in the early seventeenth century that narrated an individual's move from sinful life to religious commitment. As many critics on spiritual autobiographies have noted, the form of the 'conversion narrative' was markedly formulaic:

> Spiritual autobiography is highly intertextual, 'determined' in large part by previous self-portraits, and 'governed' by hermeneutics as much as by history. The operations of sin, calling, crisis, conversion, relapse, confession, prayer and apology are the interpretive and narrative 'structures' into which spiritual autobiographers primarily fit their varied experience. Their lives are thus not entirely their own; their histories are already significantly 'bound'.[36]

The performative and visceral elements of identity are demonstrated in Orwell's *A Clergyman's Daughter*, in which the protagonist Dorothy loses her faith. At the end of the novel she is still serving church life by making costumes for the church pageant. She dwells on her newly atheist state:

> Where had she gone, that well-meaning ridiculous girl who had prayed ecstatically in summer-scented fields and pricked her arm as a punishment for sacrilegious thoughts? And where is any of ourselves of even a year ago? And yet after all – and here lay the trouble – she *was* the same girl. Beliefs change, thoughts change, but there is some inner part of the soul that does not change. Faith vanishes, but the need for faith remains the same as before. (V. ii)

Orwell asserts continuity over time in the 'soul', utilizing religious vocabulary for his atheist character, as well as locating ecstatic prayer in the English landscape. Dorothy yearns for faith and prays for belief but finds it 'useless, absolutely useless'. But, Orwell notes:

> The smell of glue was the answer to her prayer. She did not know this. She did not reflect, consciously, that the solution to her difficulty lay in accepting the fact there was no solution; that if one gets on with the job that lies to hand, the ultimate purpose of the job fades into insignificance; that faith and no faith are very much the same provided that one is doing what is customary, useful and acceptable. She could not formulate these thoughts as yet, she could only live them. (V. ii)

Orwell reveals the unacknowledged effect of actions on the individual. Rituals – of 'faith and no faith' – are visceral and constitutive of the self in a way that unsettles the rationalist agenda.[37] Despite the ubiquity of ritual (we are all engaged in repeated activities), visible ritual is nonetheless conceptualized in Islamophobic discourse as a uniquely irrational activity.

Martin Amis's writing on Muslims is replete with reference to the Muslim's irrationality. Not only was 9/11 'a veritable Walpurgis night of the irrational' (*The Second Plane*, p. 13), but he asserts: 'The champions of militant Islam are, of course, misogynists, woman-haters; they are also misologists – haters of reason.' His assertion is structured to compel: the defence of helpless women has become a signal of the unreasonable (what Spivak has called white men protecting brown women from brown men). It is an assertion voiced repeatedly in anti-Islamic sentiment as a rally cry of justice. Nick Griffin in his infamous appearance on *Question Time* in 2010 reverts to arguments about gender equality:

> Because it treats women as second class citizens, because it says that a woman victim of rape should be stoned to death for adultery and because it orders its followers to be harsh with the unbelievers who live near them . . . There are good points about Islam, for example it opposes usury, it would not have allowed the banks to have run riot in the way the Tory party and Labour party have done, there are good points but it doesn't fit in with . . . British society, free speech, democracy and equal rights for women.[38]

Rather than providing evidence, Amis like Griffin builds upon a foundation of the stock prejudice of Muslim misogyny. Returning to Amis's hatred of Islam's ritualized religion, he represents it as 'a massive agglutination of stock response, of clichés, of inherited and unexamined formulations' (*The Second Plane*, p. 19), that invokes his own description of Christian chapel, suggesting that it is not just Islam, but all religion that Amis rejects. It is also reminiscent of Protestant rejection of Catholic ritual in its rejection of 'stock response'. Bradley and Tate go on to summarize Amis's attitude: 'the Islamist mind is "dependent" – inert, vacant, airless – and thus utterly impermeable to our logic, reason or understanding' (p. 41). The Islamist is

irrational to the degree of being beyond Western logic, and it is an
irrationality based upon 'unexamined formulations'.

Islam, for Amis, is so irrational, it is even atavistic:

> militant fundamentalism is convulsed in a late-medieval stage of
> its evolution. We would have to sit through a Renaissance and a
> Reformation, and then await an Enlightenment. And we're not
> going to do that. (p. 9)

Amis's views are reflected in a poll in which the majority assented to
the statement that Islam is 'more medieval than modern'.[39] Amis's
representation of Islamism conforms to Anne McClintock's critique
of colonizing attitudes that represent the colonized as 'prehistoric,
atavistic, and irrational, inherently out of place in the historical time
of modernity'. Such peoples are treated, McClintock explains, as
'*temporally* different and thus as irrevocably superannuated by
history'.[40] For Amis, the Enlightenment is the apotheosis of civilization and Islamists are rendered historically frozen in a pre-enlightened
past, the slippery term Islamism representing, in practical terms in
Amis's writing, all Muslims (see Bradley and Tate, pp. 42–3). He
makes McClintock's point quite explicitly: 'The conflicts we now face
or fear involve opposed geographical arenas, but also opposed centuries or even millennia' (*The Second Plane*, p. 13).

Hanif Kureishi, in *The Black Album* contrasts British-Muslim
identity, as it manifested itself over the course of the 'Rushdie affair',
to English norms and practices, outlining the binaries of Muslim
aggression, alienation and exuberance and English control, mythological belonging and reservation. The novel covers the period of the
burning of books in Bradford and narrates the story of a Muslim
who is caught between a radical Islamic group and secular atheism
(represented by his girlfriend, Deedee). The comparison between the
two cultures is expressed as between religions by the radical leader
Riaz:

> 'We're not blasted Christians,' Riaz replied with considerable
> aggression in him, though the effect was rather undermined by the
> fact that he was, as usual, carrying his briefcase. 'We don't turn the
> other cheek. We will fight for our people who are being tortured in

Palestine, Afghanistan, Kashmir! War has been declared against us. But we are armed.'[41]

But the representative of English intellectual attitude, the Cultural Studies lecturer Deedee, portrays the clash as cultural and racial. Speaking of the radicalized Chad, whose white adoptive mother rants against 'pakis', she explains his sense of alienation from the country of his birth:

Chad would hear church bells. He'd see English country cottages and ordinary English people who were secure, who effortlessly belonged. You know, the whole Orwellian idea of England. (p. 106)

Deedee suggests a visceral attachment to place in which belonging is mediated by literary mythologies of place. Although it is illogical that the lives of the 'ordinary English people' that Chad sees correspond to the Orwellian church bells and cottages, there is a sense that the mythology is actuated in a way to hinder Chad's appropriation of Englishness. The myth, though not corresponding to reality, demands an assent to heritage that can be appropriated by the 'ordinary English' in a way that is impossible for Chad.

Kureishi explicitly posits the expressiveness of Muslims of the novel against English reserve. The protagonist Shahid notes his own shock at the 'intimacy' of a remark by the radical leader, Riaz, and considers it a result of his English context: 'Perhaps Shahid had been among too many undemonstrative English people lately' (p. 4). The opposition of expression and repression is played out in a more extreme form in Martin Amis's 'Terror and Boredom: The Dependent Mind' (first published in September 2006 in *The Observer*). He claims here that the political self-control of Western youth is due to the channelling of dangerous impulses into alcohol, unrestricted diet, 'powerful and expensive machines', more alcohol, 'additional stimulants and relaxants', 'jumping up and down' on 'dancefloors' and 'by having galvanic sex with near-perfect strangers'. Painting a picture of youth as a dangerous mass of impulses, he notes that 'These diversions were not available to the young men of Peshawar' (*The Second Plane*, p. 47). Amis's representation of the sexually frustrated Muslim (also hardly complementary to Western youth) is fairly representative of a construction of Muslims as emotionally and sexually uncontrolled, that is an outworking of their oppositional status to the safe English gentleman who has full control of all passions, with his 'stiff upper lip'. It is a viewpoint reflected in the polls in which a significant minority identify Muslims as 'fanatical' or 'immoderate'.[42] In the EDL article 'Al Quds March London 2010', the author narrates a march by EDL's 'Jewish Division' and 'Gay Division' 'proving once again that these movements are not racial, they are ideological', in which Islam is represented as 'A religion that promotes violence against non believers this induces certain Muslims into a rabid frenzy, these Muslims must be challenged wherever they raise their evil heads.' The reasonableness of limited and specific criticism (against only 'certain Muslims') is belied by the inflammatory phrase 'rabid frenzy' and by the later statement: 'but then do you expect anything less from a religion who's [sic] disciples want a mosque at Ground Zero? Respect isn't exactly their strongpoint'.[43]

Lascivious and seething, the Muslim's lack of control – a quality the English repeatedly congratulate themselves for – is also expressed in fears of Muslim fecundity. The dangers of the uncontrolled body of the Muslim extend into the perceived uncontrolled *bodies* of Muslims. Amis, again, is representative in his convoluted warning against being 'out-bred' by Muslims (*The Second Plane*, p. 157). He asserts: 'They're also gaining on us demographically at a huge rate. A quarter of humanity now and by 2025 they'll be a third. Italy's down to 1.1 child per woman. We're going to be outnumbered.'[44] Anticipating Lord Pearson's new role as leader of the UK Independence Party, *The Times* printed his 'outspoken views' on Islam, made in Washington DC in October 2009, which were focused primarily on demographic takeover:

> The fact that Muslims are breeding ten times faster than us. I do not know at what point they reach such a number that we are no longer able to resist the rest of their demands . . . but if we do not do something now within the next year or two we have in effect lost.[45]

Pearson points to the 'breeding' of Muslims but also paints them as an inexhaustible set of needs, with 'the rest of their demands', constructing an overall picture of uncontrollable impulses. Charles

Moore, editor of *The Spectator Magazine* wrote on 19 October 1991 in his article 'Time for a More Liberal and "Racist" Immigration Policy' that:

Because of our obstinate refusal to have enough babies, Western European civilisation will start to die at the point when it could have been revived with new blood. Then the hooded hordes will win, and the Koran will be taught, as Gibbon famously imagined, in the schools of Oxford.[46]

Demographic dangers are replicated in the urban threat of Muslims to the ideal of rural England and the simplicity, honesty and authenticity that it represents. Englishness as expressed in the simple, rural life has as its counterpart the long established equation of the Muslims with urban space. John Ruskin's lament over 'crowded tenements' is focused on the transformation of the urban Englishman into an 'Arab' or 'Gypsy'.[47] If the English icon is the countryside, then that ascribed to the Muslim is the 'second plane' of Amis's book. Muslims are thereby urban: the second plane's impact with the tower, while primarily iconic of a terrorism that used Islam as an excuse, also invokes Muslim urbanity. The image is a palimpsest of *the* two towers that overlays the iconic representation of Muslim states such as Dubai that are both modern and ostentatious. Recent research by Bridget Byrne on the attitudes of white mothers living in London underlines both the force of nostalgic mythologies of England on their attitudes and, among other things, the urbanized nature of Muslims. One interviewee contrasts the 'little village shop in the country' and her own urban 'nice road' with 'lots of light', with degraded Muslim urbanity:

But I wouldn't go shopping in some of the shops. Have you walked round here at all? . . . if you go round the back there are some, in the market place you get all this halal meat and all sorts of stuff. I wouldn't touch that with a barge pole. Not because it's different, or because of anything. But just because I think it smells funny.[48]

The Muslim urban spaces are 'round the back', a separate and claustrophobic space that contrasts with the 'nice road' marked by light. Both sites carry suggestive moral associations of closedness and openness. As well as the explicit comparison of village and a marred urban lifestyle, there is also an implicit comparison of rural animal welfare (in the 'grassy plains' that the interviewee earlier speaks of, an exceptionally open descriptor) and halal practices. The interviewee's response, notably, is articulated in visceral terms – her repulsion is based not in a rational explanation of the problems of the shops, halal meat and the strikingly vague 'all sorts of stuff' but in her assertion that 'I think it smells funny'. Bodily revulsion, yet again, presents the final say in aversion to Muslim practices.

Anti-Islamic sentiment is unarguably at times a conscious, rational and chosen prejudice. What this chapter has tried to argue is that while conscious adherence to prejudice is apparent, less obvious is the grounding of an unconsciously perpetuated antagonism that resides in the habitual activities, tastes, dispositions and materialities of Englishness. Anti-Islamic sentiment overwhelmingly mirrors those English characteristics grounded in simplicity: the Muslim as ostentatious in dress and ritual; as irrational and as dangerously uncontrolled. The fact that anti-Islamic sentiment reflects these English characteristics suggests Islamophobia, at least in part, is a by-product of the seemingly innocent mythology of English simplicity.

* * *

The interviewee just discussed posits her sense of Englishness explicitly in literature:

> I sort of consider English and things sort of like *Howard's End* and that kind of thing. And I think there's something, I mean I know it's 200 years ago or whatever, but I think there's something wonderful about all that. (p. 517)

What Byrne calls a 'novelised experience' (p. 517) is replicated in Scruton's construction of a literary heritage that 'enchants' the landscape and its inhabitants. While literature's place in the mythologies of Englishness is widely recognized, the importance of religion has been neglected, its presence in secular articulations of Englishness considered anachronistic. And yet the sentimental and visceral attachment to national identity and place is suggestive of the workings of faith. To attenuate religious and national identities into the irrational and rational is a category mistake. While religion is assumed to be irrational, Protestant simplicity instead sublimates the rational. And whereas the nation-state is a political legal entity, national identity posited by many as a conscious act of chosen affiliation, personal attachment to the nation is perpetuated through visceral, habitual activity that continues at an unconscious level.

Simplicity is a deceptive quality. Its very nature expresses lack of guile and contradiction. It is a guarantor of meaning. Pared down, unfettered and offering full disclosure, it appeals to a desire for foundations and truth. Attention to the historical significance of simplicity reveals its origins in the oppositional and elect logics of Protestant hermeneutics and aesthetics. Simplicity and its seemingly innocent and self-evident qualities of straightforwardness, honesty and authenticity are permeated with Reformation assumptions about transparency and primacy. English aesthetics of simplicity are naively considered to hold positive moral value, which means the non-simple are judged negatively. Functioning as it does on an unconscious level, can the negative significance of simplicity – with its freight of oppositional superiority – be dislocated from the positive qualities of love of home, of landscape, honesty and reasonableness? If Barthes' insistence on the durability of myths is to be believed, then English simplicity will continue to fuel its aesthetic prejudices. Yet, aversion to what is seen as non-simple, elaborate and overly complex may be tempered if (as this book has tried to argue) the simple – and especially English simplicity – is recognized to be far from straightforward.

NOTES

INTRODUCTION

1. Frances Hodgson Burnett, *The Secret Garden* (London and New York: Penguin, 2002 [1911]). All further references will be given in the text.
2. See Robert Colls, *Identity of England* (Oxford: Oxford University Press, 2002), p. 205 and David Gervais, *Literary Englands: Versions of 'Englishness' in Modern Writing* (Cambridge: Cambridge University Press, 1993), p. 5.
3. Zygmunt Bauman, *Modernity and the Holocaust* (Cambridge: Polity Press, 1989), p. 65.
4. For books on colonial relationship, see Ian Baucom, *Out of Place: Englishness, Empire and the Locations of Identity* (Princeton, NJ: Princeton University Press, 1999), Simon Gikandi, *Maps of Englishness: Writing Identity in the Culture of Colonialism* (New York: Columbia University Press, 1996), Krishnan Kumar, *The Making of English Identity* (Cambridge: Cambridge University Press, 2003) and Graham MacPhee and Prem Poddar, *Empire and After: Englishness in Postcolonial Perspective* (Oxford: Berghahn Books, 2007). Studies published in just the last six years include: Arthur Aughey, *The Politics of Englishness* (Manchester: Manchester University Press, 2007), Christine Berberich, *The Image of the English Gentleman in Twentieth-Century Literature: Englishness and Nostalgia* (Aldershot: Ashgate, 2007), Robert Burden and Stephan Kohl, *Landscape and Englishness*, Spatial Practices, vol. 1 (Amsterdam and New York: Rodopi, 2006), Simon Featherstone, *Englishness: Twentieth-Century Popular Culture and the Forming of English Identity* (Edinburgh: Edinburgh University Press, 2009), Kate Fox, *Watching the English: The Hidden Rules of English Behaviour* (London: Hodder and Stoughton, 2004), Ina Habermann, *Myth, Memory and Middlebrow: Priestley, du Maurier and the Symbolic Form of Englishness* (Basingstoke: Palgrave Macmillan, 2010), Cole Moreton, *Is God Still an Englishman?: How We Lost Our Faith but Found a New Soul* (London: Little, Brown, 2010). For a list of key books previous to 2006, see note 1 in Bridget Byrne, 'England – whose England?: Narratives of Nostalgia, Emptiness and Evasion in Imaginations of National Identity', *The Sociological Review* 55.3 (2007), 509–30 (p. 528).
5. For the coining of 'Englishness' see Paul Langford, *Englishness Identified: Manners and Character 1650–1850* (Oxford: Oxford University Press, 2000), p. 1.

6. A. D. Smith calls the modernist position the 'dominant orthodoxy in the field', in *Nationalism and Modernism: A Critical Survey of Recent Theories of Nations and Nationalism* (London and New York: Routledge, 1998), p. xii, and its main proponent is Ernest Gellner, *Nations and Nationalism* (Oxford: Blackwell, 1983), (who denies the importance of early formations of national identity in his debate with Smith, see 'The Nation: Real or Imagined?: The Warwick Debates' at <http://www.lse.ac.uk/Depts/Government/gellner/Warwick0.html> accessed 10 December 2010).

7. See Adrian Hastings, *The Construction of Nationhood: Ethnicity, Religion and Nationalism*, The 1996 Wiles Lectures given at The Queen's University of Belfast (Cambridge: Cambridge University Press, 1997), Liah Greenfeld, *Nationalism, Five Roads to Modernity* (Cambridge, MA and London: Harvester Press, 1992), and Anthony Smith, 'Ethnic Election and National Destiny: Some Religious Origins of Nationalist Ideals', in *Nations and Nationalism* 5.3 (1999), 331–55.

8. John Fowles, 'On Being English, but not British', *Texas Quarterly* 7 (1964), 154–62 and Kumar, *The Making of English Identity*.

9. Jeremy Paxman, *The English* (London: Penguin, 1998), p. 23.

10. 'Is God Still and Englishman? Asks Cole Moreton', 10 April 2010, *Mail Online* <www.dailymail.co.uk>, accessed 27 July 2010.

11. 'Archbishop's speech on Englishness', The Sunday Times Literary Festival, 4 April 2009, at <www.archbishopofyork.org/2369?9=asks>. The bulk of this speech was reprinted as 'Celebrating Englishness does not mean you are B.N.P', *The Sun*, 7 April 2009, implying that Sentamu's unarguably conservative stance here is one that appeals to *Sun* and *Times* readers.

12. Roger Scruton, *England: An Elegy* (Chatto & Windus, 2000; London: Continuum, 2006), p. 5. All further references will be in the text. Scruton writes of what is often called the 'Nairn-Anderson theses' published in *New Left Review* in the 1960s. Anderson admits to his own 'indiscrimate rejection of English cultural traditions' in *English Questions* (London and New York: Verso 1992), p. 4.

13. Max Weber, *The Protestant Ethic and the Spirit of Capitalism* (London and New York: Routledge, 2007 [1930]). Hans Blumenberg in *The Legitimacy of the Modern Age*, trans. by Robert M. Wallace (Cambridge, MA: MIP Press, 1985), has argued against modernity's cultural debt to Christianity, a debt asserted in secularization theories such as that of Charles Schmitt in *Political Theology: Four Chapters on the Concept of Sovereignty*, trans. by George Schwab (Chicago: University of Chicago Press, 2005). For an overview of the debate between Blumengberg and Schmitt see Pini Ifergan, 'Cutting to the Chase: Carl Schmitt and Hans Blumenberg on Political Theology and Secularization', *New German Critique* 111, 37.3 (2010), 149–71.

14. George Orwell, *The English People* (London: Collins, 1947), p. 14.

15. Schmitt argues, for example, that 'all the significant concepts of the modern doctrine of the state are secularized theological concepts', *Political Theology*, p. 36. Although Taylor considers art in relation to the

transcendent, his overall focus is conceptual in his *The Secular Age* (Cambridge, MA and London: The Belknap Press of Harvard University Press, 2007).

16. For example, Michael Billig who focuses on 'ideological habits' in *Banal Nationalism* (London: Sage, 1995), p. 6, but veers towards a focus on 'widespread and common habits of thinking' (p. 9) and Jon Fox and Cynthia Miller-Idriss in 'Everyday Nationhood', *Ethnicities* 8 (2008), 536–63, who analyse, among other things, 'performing' the nation.

17. Linda Colley, *Britons: Forging the Nation, 1707–1937* (New Haven and London: Yale University Press, 1992), Liah Greenfeld, *Nationalism*, Smith, 'Ethnic Election and National Destiny' and Hans Kohn, *The Idea of Nationalism: A Study in its Origins and Background* (New York: The Macmillan Company, 1945).

18. Unlike many who assert it as common knowledge, Clement Fatoviç offers convincing textual evidence regarding Republican and Liberal debts to an anti-Catholic Protestantism, from which he argues that 'the roots of individualism are firmly planted in the soil of Protestant theology', in 'The Anti-Catholic Roots of Liberal and Republican Conceptions of Freedom in English Political Thought', *Journal of the History of Ideas* 66.1 (2005), 37–58 (p. 45).

19. Nancy Armstrong and Leonard Tennenhouse question the assertion of a rational individual in these terms in the early modern period, see *The Imaginary Puritan: Literature, Intellectual Labor, and the Origins of Personal Life,* The New Historicism: Studies in Cultural Poetics (Berkeley: University of California Press, 1992).

20. See John M. Mackenzie, *Orientalism: History, Theory and the Arts* (Manchester and New York: Manchester University Press, 1995), p. 11.

21. Crispin Sartwell, *Political Aesthetics* (Cornell University Press, 2010), p. 203.

22. For Hill's argument see *The English Bible and the Seventeenth Century Revolution* (London: Penguin, 1993).

23. Key works that discuss the new Protestant aesthetics of plainness are William A Dyrness, *Reformed Theology and Visual Culture: The Protestant Imagination from Calvin to Edwards* (Cambridge: Cambridge University Press, 2004) and Peter Auksi, *Christian Plain Style: The Evolution of a Spiritual Idea* (Montreal and Kingston: McGill-Queen's University Press, 1995) whose European focus notes the continuity not transformation of the significance of simplicity at the Reformation.

24. See Herbert L. Kessler, 'Image and Object: Christ's Dual Nature and the Crisis of Early Medieval Art', *The Long Morning of Medieval Europe: New Directions in Early Medieval Studies*, ed. by Jennifer R. Davis and Michael McCormick (Aldershot: Ashgate Publishing, 2008), pp. 291–320.

25. Peter Auksi, *Christian Plain Style*, p. 168.

26. See Peter Weigel, *Aquinas on Simplicity: An Investigation into the Foundations of his Philosophical Theology* (Bern: Peter Lang, 2008).

27. Seen by its followers as a paradigm shift, there were of course continuities in the concept of simplicity. See the discussion, for example, in

Christopher Ocker's *Biblical Poetics before Humanism and Reformation* (Cambridge: Cambridge University Press, 2002), especially pp. 112–18.

28. John N. King, *Spenser's Poetry and the Reformation Tradition* (Princeton, NJ: Princeton University Press, 1990), p. 82. All further references will be given in the text.

29. See Pasi Ihalainen, *Protestant Nations Redefined: Changing Perceptions of National Identity in the Rhetoric of the English, Dutch and Swedish Public Churches, 1685–1772* (Leiden: Brill, 2005), pp. 20–1 and chapter 5.

30. Edmund Spenser, *The Faerie Queene*, ed. by A. C. Hamilton with Hiroshi Yamashita, Toshiyuki Suzuki and Shohachi Fukunda, Longman Annotated Poets, rev. 2nd edn (London: Pearson Education Ltd., 2007). All further references will be given in the text.

31. Naomi Baker, *Plain Ugly: The Unattractive Body in Early Modern Culture* (Manchester: Manchester University Press, 2010), pp. 72–3.

32. Martin Luther, *A commentarie vpon the fiftene Psalmes*, trans. by Henry Bull (printed by Thomas Vautroullier, 1577). EEBO accessed 12 July 2010.

33. See John N. King and Mark Rankin, 'Print, Patronage, and the Reception of Continental Reform', *Yearbook of English Studies* 38.1–2 (2008), 49–67.

34. Jean Calvin, *The Sermons of M. Iohn Calvin, vpon the Epistle of S. Paule too the Ephesians*, trans. by Arthur Golding (London, 1577). EEBO, accessed 14 June 2010.

35. Thomas H. Luxon, *Literal Figures: Puritan Allegory and the Reformation Crisis in Representation* (Chicago and London: The University of Chicago Press, 1995), p. 24. All further references will be given in the text.

36. Burkart Holzner and Leslie Holzner have posited the emergence of transparency at the Reformation. They identify a link between 'Protestantism and early support for transparency (but always in what we have called "bounded" ways)' (p. 21). Their focus is on the political sphere and the revolution against corruption that led to 'prototransparency', in other words recognition of the need for openness in communication. 'The idea of sanctity of conscience and of humanity's direct, personal bond to God had already appeared in some movements in the Middle Ages', they note, but it was Protestantism that 'spread these ideas as a main source of faith to very large populations of central and northern Europe' (p. 19). Although positing transparency as an outcome of Reformation theological ideas, it is a political idea (transparency between state and subjects, between individuals), and not related to changes in aesthetics. *Transparency in Global Change: The Vanguard of the Open Society* (Pittsburgh: University of Pittsburgh Press, 2006).

37. John Bale *The Image of Bothe Churches after Reulacion of saynt Iohan hte euangelyst* (1545). EEBO, accessed 27 June 2010. All further references will be given in the text.

38. 'Letter to Raleigh', in Spenser, *The Faerie Queene*, p. 714.

39. For a discussion of the changing conceptualization of the relation between outer and inner states in the early modern period, see Naomi Baker, *Plain Ugly*, especially chapter 1.
40. Claire McEachern, *The Poetics of English Nationhood, 1590–1612*, Cambridge Studies in Renaissance Literature and Culture 13 (Cambridge: Cambridge University Press, 1996), p. 12.
41. For an account of Protestant England's internalization of imagery, see Dyrness, *Reformed Theology*, chapter 7.
42. Dyrness, p. 6. He primarily discusses aesthetics in the outworking of Reformed theologies in the specific English genres of portraiture and landscape painting.
43. Northrop Frye, *The Secular Scripture: A Study of the Structure of Romance* (Boston: Harvard University Press, 1976).
44. John Milton, *Paradise Lost*, ed. by Alastair Fowler, Longman Annotated Poets, rev. 2nd edn (London: Pearson Education Ltd., 2007). All further references will be given in the text.
45. On the privatization of religion in the secular nation, see Julia Kristeva, *Nations without Nationalism*, trans. by Leon S. Roudiez (New York: Columbia University Press, 1993).
46. N. T. Madan, 'Secularism in its Place', *The Journal of Asian Studies* 46.4 (1987), 747–59 (p. 748).
47. Barthes explains: 'Myth [. . .] is a language which does not want to die: it wrests from the meanings which give it its sustenance an insidious, degraded survival, it provokes in them an artificial reprieve in which it settles comfortably, it turns them into speaking corpses' in *Mythologies*, trans. by Annette Lavers and Siân Reynolds (London: Vintage Books, 2009 [1972]), p. 158. All further references will be given in the text.
48. See, for example, Jacques Derrida, 'Faith and Knowledge: The Two Sources of "Religion" at the Limits of Reason Alone', in *Acts of Religion*, ed. by Gil Anidjar (New York and London: Routledge, 2002), pp. 40–101.
49. See, for example, the discussion in Marcus Walsh, 'Profession and Authority: The Interpretation of the Bible in the Seventeenth and Eighteenth Centuries', *Literature and Theology* 9.4 (1995), 383–98 (p. 384).
50. Edward Said, *Culture and Imperialism* (London: Vintage, 1994), p. xiii.
51. J. B. Priestley, *English Humour* (London: Longmans, Green and Co., 1929), p. 9. All further references will be given in the text.
52. See, for example, the excellent Timothy Rosendale, *Liturgy and Literature in the Making of Protestant England* (Cambridge: Cambridge University Press, 2007).
53. See John R. King, *Milton and Religious Controversy: Satire and Polemic in Paradise Lost* (Cambridge: Cambridge University Press, 2000), p. 25.
54. Benedict Anderson, *Imagined Communities: Reflections on the Origins and Spread of Nationalism* (London: Verso 1991, repr. 1995 [1983]).
55. Raymond Williams, *The Long Revolution* (London: Penguin, 1961), p. 65. On 'structures of feeling' see pp. 64–88.
56. Louis Althusser, 'A Letter on Art in Reply to André Daspre', in *Lenin and Philosophy and Other Essays* (New York and London: Monthly

Review Press, 2001), p. 152. All further references will be given in the text.

57. Louis Althusser, 'Ideology and Ideological State Apparatus (Notes Towards an Investigation'), *Lenin and Philosophy*, p. 96.

58. William Shakespeare, *King Richard II*, ed. by Charles R. Forker (London: Arden Shakespeare, 2005), II. i. 43. Paul Schwyzer argues that the geographical description points to a British construction of English identity, see *Literature, Nationalism, and Memory in Early Modern England and Wales* (Cambridge: Cambridge University Press, 2004), p. 4.

59. The distinction is made by Christopher, G. Flood in *Political Myth* (New York and London: Routledge, 2002), p. 6.

60. Richard Littlejohns and Sara Soncini (eds), *Myths of Europe* (Amsterdam and New York: Rodopi, 2007), p. 15, fn 13, who explain: 'Plato advocates the state forging a mythology that is capable of "grow[ing] into habits and becom[ing] a second nature, affecting body, voice and mind"' (*Republic* 3, 395 c8–d3). All further references will be given in the text.

61. Flood similarly argues in his *Political Myth*: 'The efficacy of myth is its particular capacity to create the illusion of being natural rather than intentional. A soon as the illusion is revealed, the myth is shattered' (p. 165).

62. Manfred Pfister, 'Europa/Europe: Myths and Muddles', in Littlejohns and Soncini, *Myths of Europe*, pp. 21–34 (p. 28).

63. 'Ideology and Ideological State Apparatuses', in *Lenin and Philosophy*, p. 114.

64. Pierre Bourdieu, *The Logic of Practice*, trans. by Richard Nice (Stanford, CA: Stanford University Press, 1990), p. 18. All further references are given in the text.

65. Joseph Addison, No. 409, in *The Spectator*, 8 vols (London, 1713 [1711–12]), vol. 6, p. 75.

66. Addison, No. 447, in *The Spectator*, vol. 6, p. 276. All further references will be given in the text.

67. *The Mill on the Floss*, ed. by Gordon S. Haight, Intro. by Dinah Birch (Oxford: Oxford University Press, 2008), ch. 1.

CHAPTER 1

1. See King, *Spenser's Poetry*, especially ch. 2.
2. See King, *Spenser's Poetry*, p. 71.
3. David Norbrook, *Poetry and Politics in the English Renaissance* (Oxford: Oxford University Press, rev ed., 2002), p. 99.
4. The phrase potentially identifies Fidelia's book as that of the biblical Revelation (which Bale sees as the Bible in miniature and is identified in the Geneva Bible's Peter 3.16 as 'among the which some things are hard to be vnderstand').
5. 'Letter to Raleigh', in Spenser, *The Faerie Queene*, p. 714.
6. See Naomi Baker, *Scripture Women* (Nottingham: Trent Editions, 2005). Thanks to Naomi for discussions of Thurgood's significance here. See

Naomi Baker, 'The Devil and the Debt Bill: Poverty, Theology and the Self in Rose Thurgood's "A Lecture of Repentance" (1636–7)', *Literature and Theology* 17.3 (2003), 324–40.

7. Philip Sidney, *An Apology for Poetry: or The Defence of Poesy*, ed. by R. W. Maslen, 3rd edn (Manchester: Manchester University Press, 2002), p. 86.

8. In Calvinism, as Catharine Randall outlines: ' "modesty" and "simplicity" oppose "license," "caprice," "error,", "useless things" and "confusion" ', demonstrating the complexity of simplicity as a sign, *Building Codes: The Aesthetics of Calvinism in Early Modern Europe* (Philadelphia: University of Pennsylvania Press, 1999), p. 3.

9. See discussion in Linda Gregerson, *The Reformation of the Subject: Spenser, Milton and the English Protestant Epic* (Cambridge: Cambridge University Press, 1995), p. 4. All further references will be given in the text.

10. The poem eschews ornament, 'polish'd pillars, or a roofe of gold' (l.3) to favour instaed 'soyle', 'ayre', 'wood' and 'water' (ll. 7, 8), in *The Forrest*, in *The Works of Benjamin Ionson* (1616), p. 819. EEBO, accessed 24 July 2010.

11. John Calvin, *The Institution of the Christian Religion* (London: Reinolde Wolfe & Richarde Harison, 1561). EEBO, accessed 27 June 2010.

12. Adrian Hastings, *The Construction of Nationhood*, p. 18.

13. Richard Heyrick, *Queen Esthers Resolves: Or, A Princely Pattern of Heaven-born Resolution, for all the Lovers of God and their Country: Opened in a Sermon Preached Before the Honourable House of Commons, at the Monethly Fast, May 27, 1646* (London, 1646), p. 25. EEBO, accessed 25 June 2010.

14. Hans Kohn, *The Idea of Nationalism*, p. 136.

15. Johannes Brenz, *A Right Godly and Learned Discourse Upon the Booke of Ester Most Necessary for this Time and Age, to Enstruct all Noble Men* (London, 1584), n. p. [p. 139].

16. Stockwood, John, 'Preface', in Brenz, *A Right Godly and Learned Discourse*, n. p. [p. vi].

17. See my discussion of Brentz and Stockwood in Jo Carruthers, 'Nationalism', in *The Blackwell Companion to the Bible and Culture*, ed. by John Sawyer (Oxford: Blackwell, 2006), pp. 480–96, especially. pp. 487–91.

18. Frank Kermode, 'The Element of Historical Allegory' (1964) in *Spenser, The Faerie Queene, A Casebook*, ed. by Peter Bayley (Basingstoke: Macmillan, 1977), pp. 197–210 (p. 209).

19. In *Areopagitica: A Speech of Mr. John Milton for the Liberty of Unlicens'd Printing, to the Parliament in England* (1644), p. 13, EEBO, accessed 24 June 2010. See discussion in A. C. Hamilton (ed.), *The Spenser Encyclopedia* (Toronto: University of Toronto Press, 1990), p. 366.

20. Milton, *Areopagitica*, p. 31.

21. In the fourth issue of the first edition, see Milton, *Paradise Lost*, p. 54.

22. Milton, *Paradise Lost*, pp. 54–5.

23. Joseph Lyle, 'Architecture and Idolatry in Paradise Lost', *Studies in English Literature* 40.1 (Winter 2000): 139–55. All further references will be given in the text.

24. Kermode, *The Classic: Literary Images of Permanence and Change* (Boston: Harvard University Press, 1983), p. 55.
25. John E. Knott, 'Milton's Wild Garden', *Studies in Philology* 102.1 (2005), 66–82 (p. 74) and see Charlotte F. Otten, 'My Native Element: Milton's Paradise and English Gardens', *Milton Studies* 5 (1973): 249–67. All further references will be given in the text.
26. The love of portraiture demonstrated the veneration of the mind (as seen in the eyes), Dyrness, p. 109.
27. Robert N. Watson, *Back to Nature: The Green and the Real in the Late Renaissance* (Philadelphia: University of Pennsylvania Press, 2006), p. 3, although Watson asserts a non, even anti-material Protestantism, see for example p. 38. All further references will be given in the text.
28. Aphra Behn, *Oroonoko, or The Royal Slave: A True History* (1688), pp. 166, 6, 8, EEBO, accessed 14 March 2010.

CHAPTER 2

1. Joseph Addison, No. 119, in *The Spectator*, vol. 2, p. 195.
2. Cited in 'Memorial', in Addison, *Essays, Moral and Humorous: Also Essays on Imagination and Taste* (Edinburgh: William and Robert Chambers, 1839), pp. 1–3 (p. 3). It is a simplicity that Langford traces to 'Anglo-Saxon sincerity' in his analysis of eighteenth-century plainness and manners, *Englishness Identified*, p. 88.
3. Thomas Carlyle, *Past and Present* (London: Richard Clay & Sons, 1843), p. 161.
4. Jeremy Black, *Natural and Necessary Enemies: Anglo-French Relations in the Eighteenth Century* (Atlanta: University of Georgia Press, 1986), p. 201.
5. No. 381, *The Spectator*, vol. 5, p. 363.
6. No. 85, *The Spectator*, vol. 2, p. 4. Further references will be given in the text.
7. No. 81, *The Spectator*, vol. 2, p. 6.
8. Blackwell, 1735, p. 55; cited in Fred Parker, 'Classic Simplicity', in *Translation and the Classic: Identity as Change in the History of Culture*, ed. by Alexandra Lianeri and Vanda Zajko (Oxford: Oxford University Press, 2008), pp. 227–42 (p. 229). All further references will be given in the text.
9. Raymond D. Havens, 'Simplicity, A Changing Concept', in *Journal of the History of Ideas* 14.1 (1953), 3–32.
10. F. D. Maurice, 'The Communion Service from the Book of Common Prayer, With Select Readings from the Writings of the Rev. F. D. Maurice, MA', ed. by John William Colenso, Lord Bishop of Natal (London: Macmillan and Co., 1874), vol. ii. p. 108. Project Canterbury, <http://anglicanhistory.org/maurice/colenso_communion/01.html>. Accessed 14 June 2010.
11. Nigel Yates, *Anglican Ritualism in Victorian Britain, 1830–1910* (Oxford: Oxford University Press, 1999), p. 185.

12. Shaftesbury Archives at Wimborne St Giles, SE/ NC/ 82 (3)–(4), cited Yates, pp. 186–7.
13. Alec R. Vidler, *The Church in an Age of Revolution: 1789 to the Present Day* (Harmondsworth: Penguin: 1971), p. 160.
14. Daniels, Louis E., 'The Ornaments Rubric: Its History and Force' (The Anglican Soceity, n.d.) Project Canterbury. <http://anglicanhistory.org/ liturgy/ daniels_ornaments.html>. Accessed 06 June 2010.
15. John Richard Green, *History of the English People* (London: Macmillan, 1879), iii. 13–19; his *Short History* was published in 1874; cited in Patrick Parrinder, *Nation and Novel: The English Novel from its Origins to the Present Day* (Oxford: Oxford University Press, 2006), p. 259.
16. Colin Haydon, ' "I love my King and my Country, but a Roman Catholic I hate": Anti-Catholicism, Xenophobia and National Identity in Eighteenth-century England', in *Protestantism and National Identity: Britain and Ireland, c. 1650–c. 1850* ed. by Tony Claydon and Ian McBride (Cambridge: Cambridge University Press, 2000 [1998]), pp. 33–52 (p. 40)). See also Eirwen Nicholson, 'Eighteenth-Century Foxe: Evidence for the Impact of the *Acts and Monuments* in the "Long" Eighteenth Century', in David Loades, ed., *John Foxe and the English Reformation* (Aldershot: Scolar's Press, 1997), pp. 143–77.
17. See Anthony D. Smith, *Theories of Nationalism* (London: Duckworth, 1971), p. 167.
18. King, *Milton and Religious Controversy*, p. 13. For more on Milton's heritage see Erik Gray, *Milton and the Victorians* (New York: Cornell University Press, 2009).
19. Stephen Gill, *Wordsworth and the Victorians* (Oxford: Clarendon Press, 1998). Further references will be given in the text.
20. *Book of Homilies* (London, 1647), B2, cited in Luxon, *Literal Figures*, p. 18. Stephen Prickett suggests the readerly expectation of meaning is likewise indebted to Protestant hermeneutics, retaining a cognitive focus, see *Origins of Narrative: The Romantic Appropriation of the Bible* (Cambridge: Cambridge University Press, 1996), p. 16.
21. Stanley Fish, *Surprised by Sin; The Reader in Paradise Lost* (Boston MA: Harvard University Press, 1998), p. lxxi.
22. Cited by Gill, *Wordsworth and the Victorians*, p. 3.
23. Cited in Simon Bainbridge, 'Wordsworth and Coleridge', in *The Oxford Handbook of English Literature and Theology* (Oxford: Oxford University Press, 2007), pp. 465–82 (p. 473).
24. Samuel Taylor Coleridge and William Wordsworth, *Lyrical Ballads*, ed. by Michael Mason (Harlow: Pearson Education Ltd., 2007), p. 60.
25. Letter to John Wilson, June 1802, cited in Havens, 'Simplicity', p. 28.
26. William Wordsworth, Prospectus ll. 24–5, in *The Excursion* ed. by Sally Bushell, James A. Butler and Michael C. Jaye with David Garcia (Ithaca and London: Cornell University Press, 2007), p. 39. All further references will be given in the text.
27. Samuel Taylor Coleridge, *Lectures 1795: On Politics and Religion*, ed. by Lewis Patton and Peter Mann (London: Routledge & Kegan Paul, 1987), p. 339.

28. Roger Ebbatson, *An Imaginary England: Landscape and Literature 1840–1920* (Aldershot: Ashgate, 2005), pp. 1–2.
29. Addison, No. 477, in *The Spectator*, vol. 7, p. 22.
30. John Reinhold Forster, *Observations Made During a Voyage Around the World*, ed. by Nicholas Thomas, Harriet Guest and Michael Dettelbach (Honolulu: University of Hawai'i Press, 1996 [London, 1778]), p. 182.
31. Henry Rider Haggard, *King Solomon's Mines*, ed. by Dennis Butts (Oxford: Oxford University Press, 2008), ch. 3.
32. Wordsworth's lines also implicate enclosures as a peculiarly Protestant mode of tidying and simplifying the countryside.
33. Parrinder cites Barton's statement from *Scenes of Clerical Life*, p. 37 in *Nation and Novel*, p. 269.
34. Cited in R. G. Cox, *Hardy's Critical Heritage* (London and New York: Routledge, 1979), p. 50.
35. Ian Ousby, 'Love-Hate Relationships: Bathsheba, Hardy and The Men in *Far From the Madding Crowd*', *The Cambridge Quarterly* 10.1 (1981), 24–39 (p. 25).
36. Troy is described as devilish: 'The careless sergeant smiled within himself, and probably the devil too smiled from a loop-hole in Tophet' (ch. 36).
37. Ousby reads in Bathsheba's surname (Everdene) a reference to Eve and notes a more convincing link in the description of Oak's perspective on her when he spies on her carriage in chapter 2, 'as Milton's Satan first saw Paradise' (p. 27). Further, Boldwood names her directly at the opening of chapter 17: 'Adam had awakened from his deep sleep, and behold! there was Eve'.

CHAPTER 3

1. Pierre Nora, 'Between Memory and History', *Representations* 26 (1989), 7–24 (p. 19).
2. Orwell, *The Lion and the Unicorn: Socialism and the English Genius*, 19 February 1941, in *Orwell's England*, ed. by Peter Davison (London: Penguin, 2001), pp. 250–77 (p. 252).
3. Christine Berberich, 'This Green and Pleasant Land: Cultural Constructions of Englishness', in *Landscape and Englishness,* ed. by Robert Burden and Stephen Kohl (Amsterdam and New York: Rodopi, 2006), pp. 207–24 (p. 214).
4. Rebecca Scutt and Alastair Bonnet, *In Search of England: Popular Representations of Englishness and the English Countryside* (The Centre for Rural Economy, Working Paper 22, October 1996), p. 4. All further references will be in the text.
5. George Orwell, *Coming up for Air* (London: Penguin, 2000 [1939]), book III, chapter ii.
6. See Michael Kirkham, *The Imagination of Edward Thomas* (Cambridge: Cambridge University Press, 1986), p. 125, see further pp. 33–4 especially.
7. Edward Thomas, *The Heart of England* with coloured illustrations by H. L. Richardson (London: J. M. Dent & Co. and New York: E. P. Dutton and Co., 1906), p. 67. All further references will be given in the text.

8. See Richard Terry, *James Thomson: Essays for the Tercentenary* (Liverpool: Liverpool University Press, 2000), p. 4 and p. 11.
9. Percy Bysshe Shelley, 'Misery – A Fragment', in *The Poems of Shelley, Vol 2: 1817–1819*, ed. by Geoffrey Matthews and Kelvin Everest (London and New York: Longman, 2000), pp. 703–5.
10. E. M. Forster, *Howard's End* (London: Penguin, 1989). All further references will be given in the text.
11. Wordsworth, 'Lines Written a Few Miles above Tintern', in Samuel Coleridge and William Wordsworth, *Lyrical Ballads*, ed. by Michael Mason (London and New York: Longman, 1992), pp. 205–14 (l. 48).
12. See P. N. Furbank, *E. M. Forster: A Life, Vol. i: The Growth of the Novelist (1879–1914)* (London: Secker & Warburg, 1977), p. 47, cited in Parrinder, p. 294.
13. 'Shooting an Elephant', in *Collected Essays* (London: Secker and Warburg, 1968), pp. 15–23.
14. (George Santayana, *Soliloquies in England and Later Soliloquies* (New York: C. Scriber's Sons, 1922)), p. 34
15. John Galsworthy, *The Man of Property* (London: Penguin Classics, 2001), p. 85.
16. See Judith Butler, *Gender Trouble: Feminism and the Subversion of Identity* (London: Routledge, 1990), p. 173.
17. See especially Smith, 'Ethnic Election'.

CHAPTER 4

1. Runnymede Trust, *Islamophobia: A Challenge for Us All?* Report of the Runnymede Trust Commission on British Muslims and Islamophobia (Runnymede Trust, 1997), p. 1.
2. The quotation is taken from *Review of Ethnic Minority Initiatives: Royal Navy/Royal Marines* (Office of Public Management, 1996).
3. Elizabeth Poole, *Reporting Islam: Media Representations of British Muslims* (London: I. B. Tauris, 2002), p. 248. Madan asserts that only Protestant Christianity fits the model of privatized religion, meaning that 'Buddhists, Hindus, Muslims, or Sikhs' cannot function within a secular society, 'Secularism in its Place', p. 749.
4. Pnina Werbner, 'Essentialising Essentialism, Essentialising Silence: Ambivalence and Ambiguity in the Construction of Racism and Ethnicity', in *Debating Cultural Hybridity: Multicultural Identities and the Politics of Racism,* ed. by Werbner and Tariq Modood (London: Zed Press, 1997), pp. 226–54 (p. 244), see also Christopher Allen 'From Race to Religion: The New Face of Discrimination', in *Muslim Britain: Communities under Pressure,* ed. by Tahir Abbas (London: Zed Books, 2005), pp. 49–69 (p. 49).
5. Nasar Meer and Tariq Modood, 'Refutations of Racism in the "Muslim Question"', *Patterns of Prejudice* 43.3 (2009), 335–54 (pp. 341–2).
6. Jean-Paul Sartre, *Anti-Semite and Jew*, trans. by George J. Becker (New York: Schocken Books), p. 44.

7. See, for example, Daniel Vitkus, *Turning Turk: English Theater and the Multicultural Mediterranean, 1570–1630* (New York and Basingstoke: Palgrave Macmillan, 2003) and Nabil Matar, *Islam in Britain 1558–1685* (Cambridge: Cambridge University Press, 1998).

8. This paragraph's argument is in large part a selective summary of Vitkus's chapter 'Islam in Sixteenth- and Seventeenth-Century Europe', in *Western Views of Islam in Medieval and Early Modern Europe: Perception of Other*, ed. by David R. Blanks and Michael Frassetto (Basingstoke: Palgrave Macmillan, 1999), pp. 207–30 (p. 209). All further references will be given in the text.

9. Richard Knolles, *History of the Turks* (1603), cited in Vitkus, p. 210.

10. Christopher Marlowe, *Tamburlaine*, ed. by J. S. Cunningham (Manchester and New York, 1981, repr. 1999).

11. Gabriel Faimau notes the association of Catholic with Muslim experiences of alienation within a Protestant Britain in his 'Naming Muslims as Partners', *Journalism Studies* (15 September 2010, iFirst), 1–15.

12. Julie Spraggon, *Puritan Iconoclasm during the English Civil War*, Studies in Modern British Religious History (Woodbridge: The Boydell Press, 2003), p. 16.

13. Geneva Bible Commentary, 16:19 cited in Vitkus, p. 222.

14. Kermode 'The Element of Historical Allegory', p. 207.

15. For example, Tariq Modood's research on faith schools suggests that 'nominal Christians and agnostics/atheists were more likely to express prejudice against Muslims than committed Christians', in 'Anti-Essentialism, Multiculturalism and the "Recognition" of Religious Groups', *The Journal of Political Philosophy* 6.4 (1998), 378–99 (p. 387).

16. Allen, 'From Race to Religion', p. 50.

17. Fatoviç, 'The Anti-Catholic Roots', p. 57.

18. Martin Reisigl and Ruth Wodak, *Discourse and Discrimination: Rhetorics of Racism and Antisemitism* (London: Routledge, 2001), p. 6.

19. Edward Said, *Orientalism* (Harmondsworth: Penguin, 1978), p. 38.

20. Sevgi Kiliç, 'The British Veil Wars', *Social Politics: International Studies in Gender, State and Society* 15.4 (Winter 2008): 433–54 (p. 450). All references will be given in the text.

21. Paul Bagguley and Yasmin Hussain, 'Flying the Flag for England? Citizenship, Religion and Cultural Identity among British Pakistani Muslims', in *Muslim Britain: Communities under Pressure*, ed. by Tahir Abbas (London: Zed Books Ltd., 2005), 208–21 (p. 214).

22. Polly Toynbee, 'In Defence of Islamophobia: Religion and the State', *The Independent*, 23 October 1997.

23. Martin Amis, *The Second Plane: September 11: 2001–2007* (London: Vintage Books, 2008), p. 19. Further references will be given in the text.

24. Martin Amis, *The War Against Cliché*, p. 444, cited in Arthur Bradley and Andrew Tate, *The New Atheist Novel: Fiction, Philosophy and Polemic after 9/11* (London and New York: Continuum, 2010), p. 39. All further references to Bradley and Tate will be given in the text.

25. Bhikhu Parekh, 'Discourses on National Identity', *Political Studies* 42 (1994), 492–504 (p. 504). Interestingly, Parekh cites Scruton as an

example of an 'historically determined' approach to national identity, p. 503, fn. 16.

26. Jacques Derrida, 'Signature Event Context', in *Limited Inc* (Evanston, IL: Northwestern University Press, 1988), p. 7.

27. Bradley and Tate make a similar argument in their *New Atheist Novel* regarding all of their authors, see p. 111.

28. See Tariq Modood, 'Difference, Cultural Racism and Anti-Racism', in Pnina Werbner and Tariq Modood (eds), *Debating Cultural Hybridity*, pp. 154-72, and Dana Arnold (ed.) *Cultural Identities and the Aesthetics of Britishness* (Manchester: Manchester University Press, 2004), p. 387.

29. Clive Field, 'Islamophobia in Contemporary Britain: The Evidence of Opinion Polls', *Islam and Muslim-Christian Relations* 18.4 (2007), 447–77 (p. 456). All further references will be given in the text.

30. Field's analysis reveals that in the poll commissioned by the Islamic Society of Britain and carried out by YouGoc (G2002e), half of respondents expressed there was not very much (44%) or nothing (12%) in common between their own and the values of British Muslims. The lack of concordance between British and Muslim values is from the British Social Attitudes Survey (G-2003g) which contained 1,129 respondents. Of the 500 interviewed by TNS (G-2004e), 61% viewed Muslims as wanting to form insular communities and in a poll by NOP (G-2005c) 61% of 1,012 believed 'that most Muslims coming to the country wanted to remain distinct and not adopt a British way of life' (Field, p. 457). Field notes 'some apprehension about the intensity of Muslims' religious attachments' in polls from 2004–5: in a survey commissioned by *The Times* (G-2005b), 28% of 714 respondents 'had a concern about the presence of those with strong Muslim beliefs' (Field, p. 457). Post 7/7, 46% of 1, 854 respondents to a *Daily Telegraph* commissioned survey (G-2005g) saw Islam (per se, not Islamic fundamentalist groups) as a real threat to Western liberal democracy (and only 47% who saw it as no or little threat, Field, p. 458). Regarding values, 24% of 3, 505 (G-2005j for *The Telegraph*) saw 'the tenets of Western liberal democracy and Islam as inherently contradictory', with 27% of 1,004 (G-2005m by MORI) seeing Islam and British democratics as incompatible (as opposed to 49%). One-fifth of 1,019 respondents (and one quarter of men and C2DE groupings) expressed negativity towards Islam (G-2005p). In 2005 (G-2005g), 10% felt British Muslims were not loyal to the country and condoned or would enact terrorism; only 23% saw British Muslims as law-abiding and against the bombings. In 2006 (G-2006l) 53% thought 'Islam posed a threat to Western liberal democracy' and for 41% (G-2006g) Islamic and British democrat values were deemed incompatible. 25% felt (G2006h) Islam threatened Britain's 'way of life' (Field, p. 462).

31. Available at <http://www.telegraph.co.uk/comment/personal-view/ 3632 983/Multiculturalism-hasnt-worked-lets-rediscover-Britishness.html>. accessed 27 February 2010.

32. In a survey by Gallup (G-1990c) of 1,474 white British, only 35% believed that most Muslims could be trusted, and 61% agreed with the statement 'you cannot be too careful' (see Field, 'Islamophobia', p. 451).

NOTES

33. See Meer and Modood, 'Refutations of Racism', p. 342.
34. Field reveals that a MORI poll (G-2006-r) revealed that although only 14% of 1,023 respondents found veils frightening or intimidating, 59% agreed with Jack Straw. The rise is to 74% (in G-2006h) in 2006 from 44% in 2004 (G-2004c) for greater integration. For the 69% of 490 respondents to a NOP poll (G-2006e) who noted a cohesive Islamic identity for British Muslims, 59% felt it a 'bad thing' (Field, 'Islamophobia', p. 460).
35. See, for example, the discussion in Nasar Meer, 'Less Equal than Others', *Index on Censorship* 36: 114 (2007), 114–18, p. 115 where Meer cites the BNP leaflet distributed in West Yorkshire CPS in May 2004: 'ISLAM: Intolerance, Slaughter, Looting, Arson, Molestation of Women'.
36. Larry Sisson, 'The Art and Illusion of Spiritual Autobiography', in G. Thomas Couser and Joseph Fichtelberg (eds), *True Relations: Essays on Autobiography and the Postmodern* (Westport: Greenwood Press, 1998), pp. 102–3, cited in Baker, 'The Devil and the Debt Bill', p. 332.
37. See also my discussion of visceral religion in 'Israel Zangwill, Jewish Identity and Visceral Religion', in *Religion, Literature and the Imagination*, ed. by Mark Knight and Louise Lee (Continuum, 2010), pp. 75–86.
38. <http://www.telegraph.co.uk/news/newstopics/politics/6411261/BNP-on-BBCs-Question-Time-key-quotes.html>, accessed 08 August 2010.
39. The NOP poll (G-2001f) of 600 respondents had 68% agreement (Field, p. 453).
40. Anne McClintock, *Imperial Leather: Race, Gender and Sexuality in the Colonial Quest* (New York and London: Routledge, 1995), p. 40.
41. Hanif Kureishi, *The Black Album* (Faber and Faber, 1995), p. 82. All further references will be given in the text.
42. 48% of 490 respondents (G-2006e) described Muslims as 'fanatical' and 28% of 1, 696 (G-2006k) as 'immoderate' (Field, p. 462).
43. <www.englishdefenceleague.org>, viewed 10 September 2010.
44. 'The Voice of Experience', interview with Ginny Dougary, *The Times*, 9 September 2006.
45. David Charter, 'UKIP to target Islamic fundamentalism with leadership election', *The Times*, 27 November 2009. , accessed 14 May 2010.
46. Cited in Runnymeade, *Islamophobia*, p. 9.
47. *Works*, vol. 8, p. 227, cited in Baucom, *Out of Place*, p. 20.
48. Byrne, 'England – whose England?', p. 518.

BIBLIOGRAPHY

All biblical references are to the King James Version unless otherwise stated.

Abbas, Tahir (ed.), *Muslim Britain: Communities under Pressure* (London: Zed Books Ltd, 2005).

Addison, Joseph, *The Spectator,* 8 vols (London, 1713 [1711–12]).

—*Essays Moral and Humorous, Also Essays on Imagination and Taste* (Edinburgh: William and Robert Chambers, 1839).

Akenson, Donald Harman, *God's People: Covenant and Land in South Africa, Israel and Ulster* (Ithaca and London: Cornell University Press, 1992).

Allen, Christopher, 'From Race to Religion: The New Face of Discrimination', in Tahir Abbas (ed.), *Muslim Britain*, pp. 49–69.

—'Islamophobia and its Consequences', in *European Islam: Challenges for Public Policy and Society*, ed. by Samir Amghar, Amel Boubekeur, Michaël Emerson (Brussels: Centre for European Policy Studies, 2007), pp. 144–67.

Althusser, Louis, *Lenin and Philosophy and Other Essays* (New York and London: Monthly Review Press, 2001).

Amis, Martin, *The Second Plane: September 11: 2001–2007* (London: Vintage Books, 2008).

—'The Voice of Experience', interview with Ginny Dougary, *The Times*, 9 September 2006.

Anderson, Benedict, *Imagined Communities: Reflections on the Origins and Spread of Nationalism* (rev edn. London: Verso 1991, repr. 1995 [1983]).

Anderson, Perry, *English Questions* (London and New York: Verso, 1992).

Armstrong, Nancy and Leonard Tennenhouse, *The Imaginary Puritan: Literature, Intellectual Labor, and the Origins of Personal Life,* The New Historicism: Studies in Cultural Poetics (Berkeley: University of California Press, 1992).

Arnold, Dana (ed.), *Cultural Identities and the Aesthetics of Britishness* (Manchester: Manchester University Press, 2004).

Aughey, Arthur, *The Politics of Englishness* (Manchester: Manchester University Press, 2007).

Auksi, Peter, *Christian Plain Style: The Evolution of a Spiritual Idea* (Montreal and Kingston: McGill-Queen's University Press, 1995).

Bagguley, Paul and Yasmin Hussain, 'Flying the Flag for England? Citizenship, Religion and Cultural Identity among British Pakistani Muslims', in Tahir Abbas (ed.), *Muslim Britain*, pp. 208–21.

Bainbridge, Simon, 'Wordsworth and Coleridge', in *The Oxford Handbook of English Literature and Theology* (Oxford: Oxford University Press, 2007), pp. 465–82.

Baker, Naomi, 'The Devil and the Debt Bill: Poverty, Theology and the Self in Rose Thurgood's "A Lecture of Repentance" (1636–7)', *Literature and Theology* 17.3 (2003), 324–40.

—*Scripture Women* (Nottingham: Trent Editions, 2005).

—*Plain Ugly: The Unattractive Body in Early Modern Culture* (Manchester: Manchester University Press, 2010).

Bal, Mieke, 'Literary Canons and Religious Identity', in *Literary Canons and Religious Identity*, ed. by Bart Philipsen, Erik Borgman, Lea Vershtricht, (Aldershot: Ashgate, 2004) pp. 9–32.

Bale, John, *The Image of Bothe Churches after Reulacion of saynt Iohan the euangelyst* (1545). EEBO, accessed 27 June 2010.

Barthes, Roland, *Mythologies*, trans. by Annette Lavers and Siân Reynolds (London: Vintage Books, 2009 [1972]).

Baucom, Ian, *Out of Place: Englishness, Empire and the Locations of Identity* (Princeton, NJ: Princeton University Press, 1999).

Bauman, Zygmunt, *Modernity and the Holocaust* (Cambridge: Polity Press, 1989).

Behn, Aphra, *Oroonoko, or The Royal Slave: A True History* (1688). EEBO, accessed 14 March 2010.

Berberich, Christine, 'This Green and Pleasant Land: Cultural Constructions of Englishness', in *Landscape and Englishness,* ed. by Robert Burden and Stephen Kohl (Amsterdam and New York: Rodopi, 2006), pp. 207–24.

—*The Image of the English Gentleman in Twentieth-Century Literature: Englishness and Nostalgia* (Aldershot: Ashgate, 2007).

Bergvall, Åke, 'The Theology of the Sign: St. Augustine and Spenser's Legend of Holiness', *SEL* 33.1 (Winter, 1993), 21–42.

Billig, Michael, *Banal Nationalism* (London: Sage, 1995).

Black, Jeremy, *Natural and Necessary Enemies: Anglo-French Relations in the Eighteenth Century* (Atlanta: University of Georgia Press, 1986).

Blumenberg, Hans, *The Legitimacy of the Modern Age*, trans. by Robert M. Wallace (Cambridge, MA: MIP Press, 1985).

Book of Homilies, Book I (1547; this edition 1562), edited by Ian Lancashire, University of Toronto, <www.anglicanlibrary.org/homilies/index.htm>, accessed 07 May 2010.

Bourdieu, Pierre, *The Logic of Practice*, trans. by Richard Nice (Stanford, CA: Stanford University Press, 1990).

Bradley, Arthur and Andrew Tate, *The New Atheist Novel: Fiction, Philosophy and Polemic after 9/11* (London and New York: Continuum, 2010).

Brenz, Johannes, *A Right Godly and Learned Discourse Upon the Booke of Ester Most Necessary for this Time and Age, to Enstruct all Noble Men* (London: Iohn Wolfe for Iohn Harrison the younger, 1584).

Burden, Robert and Stephan Kohl, *Landscape and Englishness*, Spatial Practices vol. 1 (Amsterdam and New York: Rodopi, 2006).

Burnett, Frances Hodgson, *The Secret Garden* (London and New York: Penguin, 2002 [1911]).

Butler, Judith, *Gender Trouble: Feminism and the Subversion of Identity* (London: Routledge, 1990).

Byrne, Bridget, 'England – Whose England?: Narratives of Nostalgia, Emptiness and Evasion in Imaginations of National Identity', *The Sociological Review* 55.3 (2007), 509–30.

Calvin, Jean, *The Sermons of M. Iohn Calvin, vpon the Epistle of S. Paule too the Ephesians*, trans. by Arthur Golding (London, 1577). EEBO, accessed 19 February 2010.

—*The Institution of the Christian Religion* (London: Reinolde Wolfe & Richarde Harison, 1561). EEBO, accessed 27 June 2010.

Carruthers, Jo, 'Nationalism', in *The Blackwell Companion to the Bible and Culture*, ed. by John Sawyer (Oxford: Blackwell, 2006), pp. 480–96.

—'Israel Zangwill, Jewish Identity and Visceral Religion', in *Religion, Literature and the Imagination*, ed. by Mark Knight and Louise Lee (Continuum, 2010), pp. 75–86.

Cesarani, David, 'What the Muslims can Learn from Jews', *THES*, 3 September, 2004 found on <http://www.timeshighereducation.co.uk/story.asp?storycode=190959>, accessed 17 February 2010.

Charter, David, 'UKIP to target Islamic fundamentalism with leadership election', *The Times*, 27 November 2009. <www.timesonline.co.uk/>, accessed 14 May 2010.

Clarkson, Jeremy, 'We've been robbed of our Englishness', *The Sunday Times* (25 November 2007). Available online from <www.times.co.uk/tol/comment/columnists/jeremy_clarkson/>.

Claydon, Tony and Ian McBride (eds), *Protestantism and National Identity: Britain and Ireland, c. 1650–c. 1850* (Cambridge: Cambridge University Press, 2000 [1998]).

Cohen, Robert, 'The Incredible Vagueness of Being British/English', *International Affairs* (Royal Institute of International Affairs, 1944–) 76.3, Europe: Where Does it Begin and End? (July 2000), 575–82.

Coleridge, Samuel Taylor, *Lectures 1795: On Politics and Religion*, ed. by Lewis Patton and Peter Mann (London: Routledge & Kegan Paul, 1987).

—and William Wordsworth, *Lyrical Ballads*, ed. by Michael Mason, 2nd edn (Harlow: Pearson Education Ltd., 2007 [1798]).

Colley, Linda, *Britons: Forging the Nation, 1707–1937* (New Haven and London: Yale University Press, 1992).

Colls, Robert, *Identity of England* (Oxford: Oxford University Press, 2002).

Cox, R. G., *Hardy's Critical Heritage* (London and New York: Routledge, 1979).

Daniels, Louis E., 'The Ornaments Rubric: Its History and Force' (The Anglican Society, n.d.) Project Canterbury <http://anglicanhistory.org/liturgy/ daniels_ornaments.html>. Accessed 06 June 2010.

Darby, Wendy Joy, *Landscape and Identity: Geographies of Nation and Class in England* (Oxford: Berg, 2000).

Davies, C. S. L., *Peace, Print, and Protestantism, 1450–1558* (Paladin: London, 1988 [1977]).

Derrida, Jacques, *Limited Inc* (Evanston, IL: Northwestern University Press, 1988).

—'Faith and Knowledge: The Two Sources of "Religion" at the Limits of Reason Alone', in *Acts of Religion*, ed. by Gil Anidjar (New York and London: Routledge, 2002), pp. 40–101.

De Segur, Louis, Gaston A., *Plain Talk about the Protestantism of To-Day* (Charleston, SC: Bibliobazaar LLC, 2010).

Dickson, Vernon Guy, 'Truth, Wonder, and Exemplarity in Aphra Behn's Oroonoko', *SEL Studies in English Literature 1500–1900*, 47.3 (2007), 573–94.

Diehl, Huston, *Staging Reform, Reforming the Stage: Protestantism and Popular Theater in Early Modern England* (Ithaca and London: Cornell University Press, 1997).

Dodd, Philip, 'Englishness and the National Culture', in *Representing the Nation: A Reader: Histories, Heritage and Museums*, ed. by David Boswell and Jessica Evans (London and New York: Routledge, 1999), pp. 87–108.

Dyrness, William A., *Reformed Theology and Visual Culture: The Protestant Imagination from Calvin to Edwards* (Cambridge: Cambridge University Press, 2004).

Ebbatson, Roger, *An Imaginary England: Landscape and Literature 1840–1920* (Aldershot: Ashgate, 2005).

EDL, 'Al Quds March London 2010', <www.englishdefenceleague.org> accessed 10 September 2010.

Eliot, George, *Adam Bede*, ed. and Intro. by Stephen Gill (London: Penguin, 1985 [1859]).

—*Middlemarch*, ed. by Rosemary Ashton (London: Penguin, 1994, repr. 2003 [1871–2]).

—, *The Mill on the Floss*, ed. by Gordon S. Haight, Intro. by Dinah Birch (Oxford: Oxford University Press, 2008 [1860]).

Faimau, Gabriel, 'Naming Muslims as Partners', *Journalism Studies* (15 September 2010, iFirst), 1–15.

Fatoviç, Clement, 'The Anti-Catholic Roots of Liberal and Republican Conceptions of Freedom in English Political Thought', *Journal of the History of Ideas* 66.1 (2005), 37–58.

Featherstone, Simon, *Englishness: Twentieth Century Popular Culture and the Forming of English Identity* (Edinburgh: Edinburgh University Press, 2009).

Field, Clive, 'Islamophobia in Contemporary Britain: The Evidence of Opinion Polls', *Islam and Muslim-Christian Relations* 18.4 (2007), 447–77.

Finn, Margot C., *After Chartism: Class and Nation in English Radical Politics, 1848–1874* (Cambridge: Cambridge University Press, 1993).

Fish, Stanley, *Surprised by Sin: The Reader in Paradise Lost* (Boston, MA: Harvard University Press, 1998).

Fleming, James Dougal, *Milton's Secrecy and Philosophical Hermeneutics* (Aldershot: Ashgate, 2008).

Flood, Christopher, G., *Political Myth* (New York and London: Routledge, 2002).

Forster, E. M., *Howards End* (London: Penguin, 1989 [1910]).

Forster, John Reinhold, *Observations Made during a Voyage Around the World*, ed. by Nicholas Thomas, Harriet Guest and Michael Dettelbach (Honolulu: University of Hawai'i Press, 1996 [1778]).

Fowles, John, 'On Being English, but not British', *Texas Quarterly* 7 (1964), 154–62.

Fox, Jon E. and Cynthia Miller-Idriss, 'Everyday Nationhood', *Ethnicities* 8 (2008), 536–63.

—'The Here and Now of Everyday Nationhood', *Ethnicities* 8 (2008), 573–6.

Fox, Kate, *Watching the English: The Hidden Rules of English Behaviour* (London: Hodder and Stoughton, 2004).

Frye, Northrop, *The Secular Scripture: A Study of the Structure of Romance* (Boston: Harvard University Press, 1976).

Galsworthy, John, *The Man of Property* (London: Penguin Classics, 2001 [1906]).

Gellner, Ernest, *Nations and Nationalism* (Oxford: Blackwell, 1983).

—and Anthony Smith, 'The Nation: Real or Imagined?: The Warwick Debates' at <http://www.lse.ac.uk/Depts/Government/gellner/Warwick0.html> accessed 10 December 2010.

Gervais, David, *Literary Englands: Versions of 'Englishness' in Modern Writing* (Cambridge: Cambridge University Press, 1993).

Giddens, Anthony, 'Introduction' (1976) in Weber, *The Protestant Ethic and the Spirit of Capitalism,* pp. vii–xxiv.

Gikandi, Simon, *Maps of Englishness: Writing Identity in the Culture of Colonialism* (New York: Columbia University Press, 1996).

Gill, Stephen, *Wordsworth and the Victorians* (Oxford: Clarendon Press, 1998).

Gottschalk, Peter and Gabriel Greenberg, *Islamophobia: Making Muslims the Enemy* (Lanham, MD: Rowman and Littlefield Publishers, Inc., 2008).

Gray, Erik, *Milton and the Victorians* (New York: Cornell University Press, 2009).

Greenfeld, Liah, *Nationalism, Five Roads to Modernity* (Cambridge, Mass and London: Harvester Press, 1992).

Gregerson, Linda, *The Reformation of the Subject: Spenser, Milton and the English Protestant Epic* (Cambridge: Cambridge University Press, 1995).

Griffin Nick, on 'Question Time', 22 October 2009. Partial transcript available at <http://www.telegraph.co.uk/news/newstopics/politics/6411261/BNP-on-BBCs-Question-Time-key-quotes.html> accessed 08 August 2010.

Grimley, Matthew, 'The Religion of Englishness: Puritanism, Providentialism, and "National Character", 1918–1945', *Journal of British Studies* 46 (October 2007), 884–906.

Haberman, Ina, *Myth, Memory and Middlebrow: Priestley, Du Maurier and the Symbolic Form of Englishness* (Basingstoke: Palgrave Macmillan, 2010).

Haggard, Henry Rider, *King Solomon's Mines*, ed. by Dennis Butts (Oxford: Oxford University Press, 2008 [1885]).

Hamilton, A. C. (ed.), *The Spenser Encyclopedia* (Toronto: University of Toronto Press, 1990).

Hastings, Adrian, *The Construction of Nationhood: Ethnicity, Religion and Nationalism*, The 1996 Wiles Lectures given at The Queen's University of Belfast (Cambridge: Cambridge University Press, 1997).

Havens, Raymond D., 'Simplicity, A Changing Concept', in *Journal of the History of Ideas* 14.1 (1953), 3–32.

Haydon, Colin, ' "I love my King and my Country, but a Roman Catholic I hate": Anti-catholicism, Xenophobia and National Identity in Eighteenth-century England', in Claydon and McBride (eds), *Protestantism and National Identity*, pp. 33–52.

Helsinger, Elizabeth K. *Rural Scenes and National Representation : Literature in History* (Princeton, NJ: Princeton University Press, 1997).

Herbert, George, *The English Poems of George Herbert*, ed. by Helen Wilcox (Cambridge: Cambridge University Press, 2010).

Heyrick, Richard, *Queen Esthers Resolves: Or, A Princely Pattern of Heavenborn Resolution, for all the Lovers of God and their Country: Opened in a Sermon Preached Before the Honourable House of Commons, at the Monethly Fast, May 27, 1646* (London, 1646). EEBO, accessed 25 June 2010.

Hill, Christopher, *The World Turned Upside Down: Radical Ideas during the English Revolution* (London: Temple Smith, 1972).

—*The English Bible and the Seventeenth Century Revolution* (London: Penguin, 1993).

Hindmarsh, D. Bruce, *The Evangelical Conversion Narrative – Spiritual Autobiography in Early Modern England* (Oxford: Oxford University Press, 2005).

Hitchens, Christopher, 'That Blessed Plot, That Enigmatic Isle', *The Atlantic*, October 2003). <www.theatlantic.com/>, accessed 14 November 2010.

Holzner, Burkart and Leslie Holzner, *Transparency in Global Change: The Vanguard of the Open Society* (Pittsburgh: University of Pittsburgh Press, 2006).

Ifergan, Pini, 'Cutting to the Chase: Carl Schmitt and Hans Blumenberg on Political Theology and Secularization', *New German Critique* 111, 37.3 (2010), 149–71.

Ihalainen, Pasi, *Protestant Nations Redefined: Changing Perceptions of National Identity in the Rhetoric of the English, Dutch and Swedish Public Churches, 1685–1772* (Leiden: Brill, 2005).

Johnson, Ben, *The Forrest*, in *The Works of Benjamin Ionson* (1616). EEBO, accessed 24 July 2010.

Kermode, Frank, 'The Element of Historical Allegory' (1964) in *Spenser, The Faerie Queene: A Casebook*, ed. by Peter Bayley (Basingstoke: Macmillan, 1977), pp. 197–210.

—*The Classic: Literary: Literary Images of Permanence and Change* (Boston: Harvard University Press, 1983).

Kessler, Herbert L., 'Image and Object: Christ's Dual Nature and the Crisis of Early Medieval Art', *The Long Morning of Medieval Europe: New Directions in Early Medieval Studies*, ed. by Jennifer R. Davis and Michael McCormick (Aldershot: Ashgate Publishing, 2008), pp. 291–320.

Kiliç, Sevgi, 'The British Veil Wars', *Social Politics: International Studies in Gender, State and Society* 15.4 (Winter 2008), 433–54.

King, John N., *Spenser's Poetry and the Reformation Tradition* (Princeton, NJ: Princeton University Press, 1990).

—*Milton and Religious Controversy: Satire and Polemic in Paradise Lost* (Cambridge: Cambridge University Press, 2000).

King, John N. and Mark Rankin, 'Print, Patronage, and the Reception of Continental Reform', *Yearbook of English Studies* 38.1–2 (2008), 49–67.

Kirkham, Michael, *The Imagination of Edward Thomas* (Cambridge: Cambridge University Press, 1986).

Knott, John E., 'Milton's Wild Garden', *Studies in Philology* 102.1 (2005), 66–82.

Kohn, Hans, *The Idea of Nationalism: A Study in its Origins and Background* (New York: The Macmillan Company, 1945).

Kristeva, Julia, *Nations without Nationalism*, trans. by Leon S. Roudiez (New York: Columbia: Columbia University Press, 1993).

Kumar, Krishan, *The Making of English Identity* (Cambridge: Cambridge University Press, 2003).

Kureishi, Hanif, *The Black Album* (London: Faber and Faber, 1995).

Langford, Paul, *Englishness Identified: Manners and Character 1650–1850* (Oxford: Oxford University Press, 2000).

Lees-Jeffries, Hester, 'From the Fountain to the Well: Redcrosse Learns to Read', *Studies in Philology*, 100. 2 (2003), 135–76.

Littlejohns, Richard and Sara Soncini (eds), *Myths of Europe* (Amsterdam and New York: Rodopi, 2007).

Loewenstein, David and Paul Stevens, *Early Modern Nationalism and Milton's England* (Toronto, Buffalo, London: University of Toronto Press, 2008).

Luther, Martin, *A commentarie vpon the fiftene Pslames*, trans. by Henry Bull (printed by Thomas Vautroullier, 1577). EEBO, accessed 12 July 2010.

Luxon, Thomas H., *Literal Figures: Puritan Allegory and the Reformation Crisis in Representation* (Chicago and London: The University of Chicago Press, 1995).

Lyle, Joseph, 'Architecture and Idolatry in Paradise Lost', *Studies in English Literature* 40.1 (Winter 2000), 139–55.

Mackenzie, John M., *Orientalism: History, Theory and the Arts* (Manchester and New York: Manchester University Press, 1995).

MacPhee, Graham and Prem Poddar, *Empire and After: Englishness in Post-colonial Perspective* (Oxford: Berghahn Books, 2007).

Madan, N. T., 'Secularism in Its Place', *The Journal of Asian Studies* 46.4 (1987), 747–59.

Mandler, Peter, 'Against Englishness: English Culture and the Limits to Rural Nostalgia, 1850–1940', *Transactions of the Royal Historical Society* 6.7 (1997), 155–75.

Matar, Nabil, *Islam in Britain 1558–1685* (Cambridge: Cambridge University Press, 1998).

Maurice, F. D., 'The Communion Service from the Book of Common Prayer, With Select Readings from the Writings of the Rev. F. D. Maurice, MA', ed. by John William Colenso, Lord Bishop of Natal (London: Macmillan and Co., 1874), Project Canterbury, <http://anglicanhistory.org/maurice/colenso_communion/01.html>, accessed 14 June 2010.

McClintock, Anne, *Imperial Leather: Race, Gender and Sexuality in the Colonial Conquest* (New York and London: Routledge, 1995).

McEachern, Claire, *The Poetics of English Nationhood, 1590–1612*, Cambridge Studies in Renaissance Literature and Culture 13 (Cambridge: Cambridge University Press, 1996).

Meer, Nasar, 'Less Equal than Others', *Index on Censorship* 36: 114 (2007), 114–18.

—and Tariq Modood, 'The Racialization of Muslims', in *Thinking Through Islamophobia*, ed. by S. Sayyid and Abdool Karim Vakil (London: Hurst and Co., 2010), pp. 68–84.

—and Tariq Modood, 'Refutations of Racism in the "Muslim question"', *Patterns of Prejudice* 43.3 (2009), 335–54.

Milton, John, *Areopagitica: A Speech of Mr. John Milton for the Liberty of Unlicens'd Printing, to the Parliament in England* (1644). EEBO, accessed 24 June 2010.

—*Paradise Lost*, ed. by Alastair Fowler, Longman Annotated English Poets, rev. 2nd edn (London: Pearson Education Ltd., 2007).

Modood, Tariq, 'Anti-Essentialism, Multiculturalism and the "Recognition" of Religious Groups', *The Journal of Political Philosophy* 6.4 (1998), 378–99.

—'Difference, Cultural Racism and Anti-Racism', in Pnina Werbner and Tariq Modood, *Debating Cultural Hybridity*, 154–72.

Moreton, Cole, 'Is God Still and Englishman? Asks Cole Moreton', 10 April 2010, *Mail* Online. <www.dailymail.co.uk> accessed 17 July 2010.

—*Is God Still an Englishman?: How we Lost our Faith but Found a New Soul* (London: Little, Brown, 2010).

Morgan, David (ed.), *Religion and Material Culture: The Matter of Belief*, ed. by David Morgan (London and New York: Routledge, 2010).

Nicholson Eirwen, in 'Eighteenth-Century Foxe: Evidence for the Impact of the *Acts and monuments* in the "long" Eighteenth Century', in David Loades, ed., *John Foxe and the English Reformation* (Aldershot: Scolar Press, 1997), pp. 143–77.

Nora, Pierre, 'Between Memory and History', *Representations* 26 (1989), 7–24.

Norbrook, David, *Poetry and Politics in the English Renaissance* (Oxford: Oxford University Press, rev ed., 2002).

Ocker, Christopher, *Biblical Poetics before Humanism and Reformation* (Cambridge: Cambridge University Press, 2002).

Orwell, George, *Coming up for Air* (London: Penguin, 2000 [1939]).

—*The English People* (London: Collins, 1947).

—'Inside the Whale', in *Collected Essays* (London: Secker and Warburg, 1968), pp. 118–59.

—'Shooting an Elephant', in *Collected Essays* (London: Secker and Warburg, 1968), pp. 15–23.

—*The Lion and the Unicorn: Socialism and the English Genius*, 19 February 1941, in *Orwell's England*, ed. by Peter Davison (London: Penguin, 2001), pp. 250–77.

Otten, Charlotte F., ' "My Native Element": Milton's Paradise and English Gardens', *Milton Studies* 5 (1973), 249–67.

Ousby, Ian, 'Love-Hate Relationships: Bathsheba, Hardy and The Men in *Far From the Madding Crowd*', *The Cambridge Quarterly* 10.1 (1981), 24–39.

Parekh, Bhikhu, 'Discourses on National Identity', *Political Studies* 42 (1994), 492–504.

Parker, Fred, 'Classic Simplicity', in *Translation and the Classic: Identity as Change in the History of Culture* ed. by Alexandra Lianeri and Vanda Zajko (Oxford: Oxford University Press, 2008), pp. 227–42.

Parrinder, Patrick, *Nation and Novel: The English Novel from its Origins to the Present Day* (Oxford: Oxford University Press, 2006).

Paxman, Jeremy, *The English* (London: Penguin, 1998).

Pendergast, John S., *Religion, Allegory and Literacy in Early Modern England, 1560–1640: The Control of the Word* (Aldershot: Ashgate, 2006).

Pfister, Manfred, 'Europa/Europe: Myths and Muddles', in Littlejohns and Soncini, *Myths of Europe,* pp. 21–34.

Picciotto, Joanna, 'The Experimentalist Eden and *Paradise Lost*', *English Literary History* 72 (2005), 23–78.

Poole, Elizabeth, *Reporting Islam: Media Representations of British Muslims* (London: I. B. Tauris, 2002).

Prickett, Stephen, *Origins of Narrative: The Romantic Appropriation of the Bible* (Cambridge: Cambridge University Press, 1996).

Priestley, J. B., *English Humour* (London: Longmans, Green and Co., 1929).

Rambuss, Richard, 'Spenser and Milton at Mardis Gras: English Literature, American Cultural Capital, and the Reformation of New Orleans Carnival', *Boundary 2* 27.2 (2000), 45–72.

Randall, Catherine, *Building Codes: The Aesthetics of Calvinism in Early Modern Europe* (Philadelphia: University of Philadelphia Press, 1999).

Reisigl, Martin and Ruth Wodak, *Discourse and Discrimination: Rhetorics of Racism and Antisemitism* (London: Routledge, 2001).

Rosendale, Timothy, *Liturgy and Literature in the Making of Protestant England* (Cambridge: Cambridge University Press, 2007).

—'Milton, Hobbes, and the Liturgical Subject', *Studies in English Literature* 44.1 (Winter 2004), 149–72.

Runnymede Trust, *Islamophobia: A Challenge to us All?* Report of the Runnymede Trust Commission on British Muslims and Islamophobia (Runnymede Trust, 1997).

Said, Edward, *Orientalism* (Harmondsworth: Penguin, 1978).

—*Culture and Imperialism* (London: Vintage 1994).

Santayana, George, *Soliloquies in England and Later Soliloquies* (New York: C. Scribner's Sons, 1922).

Sartre, Jean-Paul, *Anti-Semite and Jew*, trans. by George J. Becker (New York: Schocken Books , 1948).

Sartwell, Crispin, *Political Aesthetics* (Ithaca: Cornell University Press, 2010).

Schmitt, Charles, *Political Theology: Four Chapters on the Concept of Sovereignty*, trans. by George Schwab (Chicago: University of Chicago Press, 2005).

Schwyzer, Paul, *Literature, Nationalism, and Memory in Early Modern England and Wales* (Cambridge: Cambridge University Press, 2004).

Scruton, Roger, *England: An Elegy* (London: Continuum, 2006 [2000]).

Scutt, Rebecca and Alastair Bonnet, *In Search of England: Popular Representations of Englishness and the English Countryside* (The Centre for Rural Economy, Working Paper 22, October 1996).

Sentamu, John, Archbishop of York, 'Archbishop's Speech on Englishness', The Sunday Times Literary Festival, Saturday 4 April 2009. <www.archbishopofyork.org/ 2369?q=asks> accessed 17 July 2010.

Shakespeare, William, *King Richard II*, ed. by Charles R. Forker (London: Arden Shakespeare, 2005).

Shelley, Percy Bysshe, 'Misery – A Fragment', in *The Poems of Shelley, Vol 2: 1817–1819*, ed. by Geoffrey Matthews and Kelvin Everest (London and New York: Longman, 2000), pp. 703–5.

Sidney, Philip, *An Apology for Poetry: or The Defence of Poesy*, ed. by R. W. Maslen, 3rd edn. (Manchester: Manchester University Press, 2002).

Simpson, David, 'Being There: Literary Criticism, Localism and Local Knowledge', *Critical Quarterly* 35.3 (1993), 3–16.

Smith, Anthony D., *Theories of Nationalism* (London: Duckworth, 1971).

—*Nationalism and Modernism: A Critical Survey of Recent Theories of Nations and Nationalism* (London and New York: Routledge, 1998).

—'Ethnic Election and National Destiny: Some Religious Origins of Nationalist Ideals', in *Nations and Nationalism* 5.3 (1999), 331–55.

—'The Limits of Everyday Nationhood', *Ethnicities* 8 (2008), 563–73.

Spenser, Edmund, *The Faerie Queene*, ed. by A. C. Hamilton with Hiroshi Yamashita, Toshiyuki Suzuki and Shohachi Fukunda, Longman Annotated Poets, rev. 2nd edn (London: Pearson Education Ltd., 2007).

Spraggon, Julie, *Puritan Iconoclasm during the English Civil War*, Studies in Modern British Religious History (Woodbridge: The Boydell Press, 2003).

Stockwood, John, 'Preface', in Brenz, *A Right Godly and Learned Discourse*.

Taylor, Charles, *A Secular Age* (Cambridge, MA and London: The Belknap Press of Harvard University Press, 2007).

Terry, Richard, *James Thomson: Essays for the Tercentenary* (Liverpool: Liverpool University Press, 2000).

Thomas, Edward, *The Heart of England* with coloured illustrations by H. L. Richardson (London: J. M. Dent & Co. and New York: E. P. Dutton and Co., 1906).

Toynbee, Polly, 'In Defence of Islamophobia: Religion and the State', *The Independent*, 23 October 1997.

Vidler, Alec R., *The Church in an Age of Revolution: 1789 to the Present Day* (Harmondsworth: Penguin, 1971).

Vitkus, Daniel J., 'Islam in Sixteenth- and Seventeenth-Century Europe', in *Western Views of Islam in Medieval and Early Modern Europe: Perception of Other*, ed. by David R. Blanks and Michael Frassetto (Basingstoke: Palgrave Macmillan, 1999), pp. 207–30.

—*Turning Turk: English Theater and the Multicultural Mediterranean, 1570–1630* (New York and Basingstoke: Palgrave Macmillan, 2003).

Walsh, Marcus, 'Profession and Authority: The Interpretation of the Bible in the Seventeenth and Eighteenth Centuries', *Literature and Theology* 9.4 (1995), 383–98.

Watson, Robert N., *Back to Nature: The Green and the Real in the Late Renaissance* (Philadelphia: University of Pennsylvania Press, 2006).

Weber, Max, *The Protestant Ethic and the Spirit of Capitalism* (London and New York: Routledge, 2007 [1930]).

Weigel, Peter, *Aquinas on Simplicity: An Investigation into the Foundations of His Philosophical Theology* (Bern: Peter Lang, 2008).

Werbner, Pnina, 'Essentialising Essentialism, Essentialising Silence: Ambivalence and Ambiguity in the Construction of Racism and Ethnicity', in Pnina Werbner and Tariq Modood, *Debating Cultural Hybridity*, pp. 226–54.

—and Tariq Modood (eds), *Debating Cultural Hybridity: Multi-Cultural Identities and the Politics of Anti-Racism* (London: Zed Press, 1997).

Williams, Raymond, *The Long Revolution* (London: Penguin, 1961).

Wordsworth, William, 'Lines Written a Few Miles above Tintern', in Coleridge, *Lyrical Ballads*, pp. 205–14.

—*The Excursion* ed. by Sally Bushell, James A. Butler and Michael C. Jaye with David Garcia (Ithaca and London: Cornell University Press, 2007).

Yates, Nigel, *Anglican Ritualism in Victorian Britain, 1830–1910* (Oxford: Oxford University Press, 1999).

INDEX